I dedicate this book to my mama and daddy who have unconditionally loved
and supported me and given me the courage to take big risks in life.

MOTHER DAUGHTER DISHES
reinventing loved classics

CHERYL NAJAFI

MY STORY

I love food. I love to talk about it, cook it, eat it and share it. For me, food starts a conversation and evokes memories.

I adore the down-home family recipes that have been passed on to me from multiple generations. They always remind me of wonderful times spent with friends and family around my mama's dinner table. These recipes inspired me to write *Mother Daughter Dishes*.

Food evolves just like we do, but we don't need to lose sight of who we are or where we come from as we change. My eating habits have changed over time and it's important that I feed my kiddos as many fresh ingredients as possible. So, I've taken my family's classic recipes and recreated a fresh, modern version of each one. I've also added a few new recipes of my own to hand down to my girls.

Although families are busier now than before, we don't have to compromise freshness and rely on processed foods to recreate family favorites. Today, fresh foods are available year-round. With this in mind, I take my mama's quick and easy meatloaf recipe, where she uses a premade soup mix for seasoning, and update it by using fresh salsa instead. Her meatloaf recipe turns into delicious sliders. The salsa gives this beloved classic a little kick, and the sliders get an enthusiastic "thumbs up" from the kids. It's the same thing, just a different presentation. Sneaky, huh?

There isn't a person in America who hasn't tasted at least one version of most of these dishes but it's my mission to update them for a generation which, I feel, needs a nudge to feel more confident in the kitchen. What better way to learn and flourish than with the foods you grew up eating? There's no mystery—you know how these recipes should taste; there's no guessing or saying, "Um, I think this is how it's supposed to taste?" Chances are, you grew up eating it!

This cookbook is a collection of dependable recipes for the everyday family.

I'm not a professional chef, just a mom, wife and friend who wants to share my recipes with you. Resurrecting these recipes has sparked a newfound joy and connection between my mom and me. Through the process of locating, studying and testing new versions of my mama's meals, stories have emerged that I had long forgotten or heard for the first time. It's my hope that this book encourages you to do the same with your mom or daughter!

CONVERSION CHART

your mama's measurements	
dash/pinch	⅛ tsp
splash	1-5 drops
scant	just barely, slightly less than
heaping	filled over the top
level	even with top, filled and leveled with a straight edge
glug	¼ cup

liquid measurements		
1 Tbsp	½ fl oz	3 tsp
2 Tbsp	1 fl oz	⅛ cup or 6 tsp
¼ cup	2 fl oz	4 Tbsp
⅓ cup	2 ⅔ fl oz	5 Tbsp + 1 tsp
½ cup	4 fl oz	8 Tbsp
⅔ cup	5 ⅓ fl oz	10 Tbsp + 2 tsp
¾ cup	6 fl oz	12 Tbsp
1 cup	8 fl oz	16 Tbsp
1 pint	16 fl oz	2 cups
1 quart	32 fl oz	2 pints
1 gallon	128 fl oz	4 qts

Live the Moment™

SUBSTITUTIONS CHART

baking powder	1 tsp	¼ tsp baking soda plus ½ tsp cream of tartar
buttermilk	1 cup	1 Tbsp lemon juice or vinegar plus enough milk to make 1 cup OR 1 cup yogurt
corn syrup (light)	1 cup	1 ¼ cups white sugar plus ⅓ cup water OR 1 cup honey
corn syrup (dark)	1 cup	¾ cup light corn syrup plus ¼ cup molasses
half-and-half	1 cup	1 cup milk plus 1 Tbsp butter
cream (heavy)	1 cup	¾ cup milk plus ⅓ cup butter
cake flour	1 cup	1 cup all-purpose flour minus 2 Tbsp
fresh herbs	1 Tbsp	1 tsp dried herbs
ketchup	1 cup	1 cup tomato sauce plus 1 tsp vinegar plus 1 Tbsp sugar
mayonnaise	1 cup	1 cup sour cream OR 1 cup plain yogurt
molasses	1 cup	¾ cup brown sugar plus 1 tsp cream of tartar
white sugar	1 cup	1 ¼ cup powdered sugar OR ¾ cup honey OR ¾ cup light corn syrup
shortening	1 cup	1 cup unsalted butter OR 1 cup margarine minus 1 tsp salt (from recipe)
sour cream	1 cup	1 cup plain yogurt OR ¾ cup buttermilk mixed with ⅓ cup butter
vinegar	1 tsp	1 tsp lemon or lime juice OR 2 tsp white wine
shallots	½ cup	½ cup red onion OR ½ cup green onion

Live the Moment™

EQUIPMENT ESSENTIALS

cutting

chef's knife
kitchen shears
paring knife
serrated bread knife
sharpening steel
cutting board

cooking

cast iron skillet
frying pans (8" & 10")
large sauté pan
roasting pan
saucepans (1 qt & 3 qt)
stock pot (5 qt & 8 qt)

baking

casserole/baking dishes (8"x8" & 9"x13")
baking sheets (heavy)
cooling rack
loaf pans
pastry blender
pastry brush
rolling pin
8" or 9" round cake pans

kitchen tools

measuring spoons
measuring cups
2 cup & 4 cup liquid measuring cups
glass mixing bowls
slotted spoons
rubber spatulas (at least 1 high-heat)
wooden spoons
kitchen tongs (long & short)
spatula/turner
can opener
corkscrew
box grater
scoops (ice cream & cookie)
thermometers (candy, meat & oven)
timer
vegetable peeler
wire strainer
colander
blender

Live the Moment℠

PANTRY MUST HAVES

oils: extra virgin olive oil, vegetable oil or canola oil, cooking spray

stocks: chicken & beef broth, bouillon

canned tomatoes: whole, diced, pureed, sauce, paste

sweeteners: granulated sugar, powdered/confectioner's sugar, brown sugar, corn syrup

baking: active dry yeast, all-purpose flour, baking powder, baking soda, chocolate chips/cocoa powder, cornmeal, cornstarch, oatmeal, pure vanilla extract, almond extract

dried herbs: basil, bay leaves, cilantro, dill, parsley flakes, oregano, rosemary, sage, thyme

spices: salt, black pepper, cinnamon, cloves, ground ginger, ground nutmeg, dried mustard, paprika, red pepper flakes, chili powder, cumin, garlic powder, onion powder

condiments: honey, ketchup, mustard, mayonnaise, peanut butter, soy sauce, white vinegar, worcestershire sauce

dry goods: dried pastas, rice, beans

Live the Moment™

BAKING TIPS

1) Unless a recipe specifically states otherwise, it is generally understood that: "eggs" means grade A, large eggs, "milk" means homogenized whole milk, "butter" means unsalted butter, "vanilla" means pure vanilla extract, "flour" means all-purpose flour.

2) Always bake with ingredients that are at room temperature. Room temperature ingredients come together easier and combine more thoroughly. To bring cold eggs to room temperature, place whole eggs into a bowl of warm water (not hot) for 10 minutes. To quickly soften butter, cut it into small pieces and arrange on a plate to sit at room temperature until softened.

3) Understand your oven. Use an oven thermometer because nearly every oven is either too hot or too cold. It is also very common for an oven to have "hot spots" or temperature variations within the oven itself. Learn your oven's unique characteristics and make adjustments to accommodate them.

4) Measure carefully when you're baking. Use standard dry measuring cups for dry ingredients and liquid measuring cups for liquids. To properly measure flour, fluff it with a spoon or whisk before measuring. Don't compact flour in the cup and level the top of the flour before adding it to the mix. Baking demands accuracy and care. It really is a science!

5) Chill your cookie dough thoroughly before you bake. Chilling the dough will allow the leavening ingredients to do their work before the butter melts and the cookies become flat.

6) Always crack an egg on a flat surface and never on the edge of the bowl. Cracking an egg on the edge of a bowl risks pushing shell fragments and the germs from the outside of the eggshell into your food. I lay a paper towel on the counter and crack the egg onto the paper towel; that way, any egg drips can be cleaned up quickly and easily.

7) Parchment paper is indispensible for lining your baking pans. It prevents all of your baked goods from sticking. It is easy to fold and cut to the correct shape and makes cleanup a snap.

8) When creaming butter and sugar, use butter that is room temperature and beat with sugar long enough to get the mixture very pale yellow and fluffy. This will take several minutes and don't rush it!

9) Don't overcrowd the oven. Keep anything you are baking as far away from the sides and as close to the center of the oven as possible. Don't place too many pans in the oven at one time and rotate your baked goods to achieve even browning. Most cakes can be rotated after 20 minutes of baking, but no sooner! Be gentle, you don't want them to fall.

10) Don't over-mix! No doubt you've come across this term in nearly every cake, cookie or muffin recipe you have ever read. But exactly what does this mean? Typically in cakes, cookies and muffins, this indicates that you should only mix until the ingredients have been incorporated and the dough/batter has achieved a uniform consistency—then stop! Don't keep stirring "just to make sure."

COOKING TIPS

1) Generally, if you would like the food you're cooking to be crispy, or if you're concentrating or reducing the items you are cooking, you would usually leave the pot uncovered. If what you're cooking will not benefit from the loss of moisture or if you want things to cook a little faster, you should consider covering the pot.

2) Drain your pasta about a minute before you think it is done and finish cooking it in the sauce. Your pasta will be more flavorful and the starch from the pasta will thicken the sauce just a little bit.

3) Taste and season as you go. This will result in what chefs call a "layering of flavors." It will usually make the difference between your dish being well-seasoned and just salty.

4) Unless you're boiling water or searing meat, you should not be using high heat. Temperature control is one of the best skills you can learn and the key is to use your ears. Usually a gentle sizzle is all you need to cook most foods. If something is popping and spattering, you can be pretty sure you need to turn down the heat.

5) Have all of your ingredients ready before you begin. Place all necessary ingredients in the workspace and do as much prep as possible before you begin cooking. This is not only the most efficient and enjoyable way to cook, but it is also the best way to make sure you have everything you need before it's too late!

6) Season your meat, fish and poultry evenly. Sprinkle your seasonings from high above the item and allow it to fall down as if it were snow. This is the best method to evenly distribute the seasonings—plus, it's fun!

7) Anytime you are trying to get a nice sear on a steak or yummy caramelization on your vegetables, make sure it is dry before adding it to the skillet. Any water on the surface will steam and you will lose the yummy brown crust that you are trying to achieve.

8) Don't overcrowd the pan! Whether you are sautéing, boiling or frying, overcrowding the pan will always result in less-than-perfect results. Use the right size pan or work in batches.

9) Most savory dishes will benefit from a pinch of sugar, and most sweet dishes will benefit from a pinch of salt. This is advice that my grandma gave me and it really seems to work.

10) If you need to add oil to something that you're frying, pour the oil around the edges of the pan. By the time it reaches the food in the center of the pan, it will be perfectly heated.

Live the Moment℠

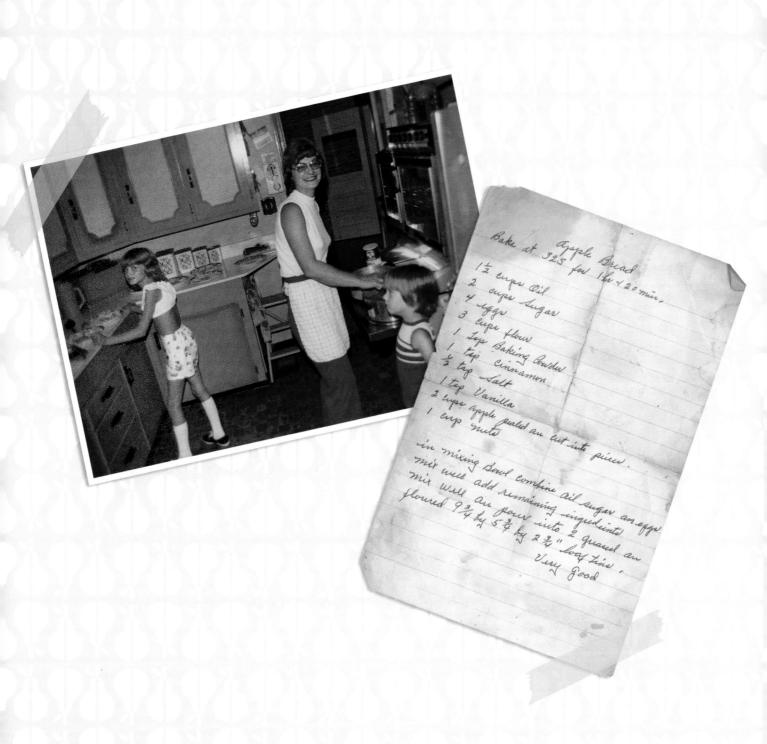

Apple Bread

Bake at 325 for 1 hr & 20 min.

1½ cups Oil
2 cups Sugar
4 eggs
3 cups Flour
1 tsp Baking Powder
½ tsp Cinnamon
1 tsp Salt
1 tsp Vanilla
2 cups apple pealed an cut into pieces.
1 cup nuts

in mixing Bowl combine oil sugar an eggs
mix well add remaining ingredients
mix well an pour into 2 greased an
floured 9¾ by 5¾ by 2¾" loaf tins.
Very good

MORNING FOODS

Breakfast is my favorite meal of the day and my favorite breakfast food is homemade biscuits. I can still smell the aroma of my Granny's freshly made biscuits filling the air in her tiny kitchen. Nothing is more mouthwatering than breaking open a hot, flaky biscuit and coating it with melted butter and dripping honey.

When I was growing up, my sister and I would spend the night with my granny and grandpa every Saturday night. We loved Saturday nights! This was an opportunity for my mama and daddy to bowl or play cards at my aunt Nancy and uncle Ron's house and it was my sister's and my time to get totally pampered.

My grandparents would pick us up Saturday afternoon and we'd go for a drive. We lived in rural Missouri, so no matter which route we took to their house, there was always something to drive by and see. I remember my grandpa taking us to see a round barn. It was more of a grain silo than a barn but round nonetheless. He would tell us the same joke every time, asking how the farmer died in the round barn. (He died running to death because he couldn't find a corner to pee in.)

My granny's go-to meal on Sunday morning was scrambled eggs, bacon and homemade biscuits. The eggs were always runny and the bacon a little too crispy for my taste, but her biscuits were wonderful. She often said, "Be careful about what you get good at or people will ask you to do it." She never enjoyed cooking, so she wasn't going to get good at it. So, if my granny can successfully do this recipe, anyone can.

opposite page: The avocado green kitchen where I learned how to cook; mama's famous apple bread recipe

EASY BUTTERMILK BISCUITS

Skip the store-bought biscuits in a can. My buttermilk biscuit recipe couldn't be easier to make or more delicious. When I prepare this recipe at home, my kids devour the entire batch in minutes!

let's do it

1 Preheat the oven to 475 degrees after placing your rack in the center of the oven.

2 Sift flour, baking powder, baking soda and salt into a large bowl. Combine the cold butter cubes with the dry ingredients then "cut" the butter into the mixture using a pastry blender or food processor. The butter particles should be about the size of a pea once you've completed the blending process.

3 Next, make a well in the middle of the flour and butter mixture then pour in buttermilk. Stir wet and dry ingredients together using a wooden spoon, combining just enough to form dough.

4 Turn the biscuit dough out onto a lightly floured surface. Sprinkle the dough lightly with flour then gently press it out with your fingers—it should be about ¾" thick.

5 Cut out the biscuits with a 3" round biscuit cutter then place the formed biscuits about 2" apart onto a greased baking sheet. Once you've cut out as many as you can, gently form the dough back into a ball and press out once again to cut as many additional biscuits as possible.

6 Bake biscuits for 10-12 minutes until they are golden brown, then remove them from the oven and allow them to cool on a rack.

7 Serve with plenty of butter, honey or jam!

 prep time: 25 minutes

 bake time: 15 minutes

makes 1 dozen biscuits

what you'll need

3 cups all-purpose flour
1 Tbsp baking powder
1 Tbsp baking soda
2 tsp salt
½ cup unsalted butter, refrigerated
    and cut into ½" cubes
1½ cups buttermilk

helpful hints

It's important to space the biscuit dough evenly on the baking sheet or they'll steam each other, keeping them from having a nice crisp texture on the outside.

People mistakenly think buttermilk contains butter because of its name but in reality, the fat has already been removed to make butter. Buttermilk is actually lower in fat than regular milk!

BUTTERMILK PANCAKES

My kiddos absolutely love a tall stack of pancakes. By placing the batter in the fridge for at least 10 minutes before cooking, or even overnight, the gluten in the mix "rests," producing extra light and fluffy pancakes.

let's do it

1 Sift the flour, sugar, salt, baking powder and baking soda into a large bowl then set aside.

2 In a separate bowl, whisk the eggs, melted butter and buttermilk together until well combined. Make a well in the center of the dry ingredients, pour the wet ingredients into the well then stir the wet and dry ingredients together until just combined. (Your batter will be slightly lumpy but don't worry! All the lumps will cook out—just be sure not to overwork the batter!)

3 Cover the bowl and refrigerate for at least 10 minutes or even overnight.

4 Heat a large non-stick skillet over medium-high heat. Brush the skillet with a little bit of oil then remove the excess with a paper towel. Pour approximately ¼-½ cup of batter into the skillet to form each pancake.

5 Cook the pancakes approximately 2-3 minutes on the first side—you'll know the pancakes are ready to flip when the outer edges are dry and bubbles pop and do not fill in. Flip the pancakes and cook an additional 1-2 minutes on the second side.

6 Repeat with remaining oil and batter. Be certain to remove any pancake bits from the skillet before beginning the next batch. Serve with plenty of warm maple syrup and enjoy!

prep time: 10 minutes
inactive prep time: 10 minutes to overnight

cook time: 5-6 minutes

makes 4 cups pancake batter

what you'll need

2 cups all-purpose flour
3 Tbsp granulated sugar
½ tsp salt
2¼ tsp baking powder
½ tsp baking soda
2 large eggs, beaten
4 Tbsp unsalted butter, melted
2 cups buttermilk, room temperature
2-3 Tbsp vegetable or canola oil

helpful hints

Don't have buttermilk? Mix 1¾ cups plus 2 Tbsp milk and 2 Tbsp of lemon juice or white vinegar. Allow mixture to sit for 2-3 minutes and you're all set to go.

Remember to wipe the oil and any leftover pancake bits from the skillet in between batches so they don't burn and cause the other pancakes to taste burnt!

APPLE BRAN MUFFINS

I love a sweet treat to start off the day, especially when it's full of healthy ingredients. I used applesauce, yogurt and bran cereal ground in a food processor to make this easy recipe moist and delicious!

let's do it

1 Preheat the oven to 375 degrees and line a muffin tin with cupcake liners or spray the pan generously with cooking spray.

2 Sift the flour, baking soda and cinnamon together in a medium-sized bowl then set aside.

3 Whisk the egg and egg yolk together in a large mixing bowl then add kosher salt, sugar, molasses and vanilla. Whisk vigorously until completely combined.

4 Then, add the melted butter, applesauce and yogurt and whisk to combine. Don't forget to scrape the sides of the bowl for every last drop!

5 Stir both the whole cereal and ground cereal into the egg mixture then let the mixture sit for approximately 5 minutes to allow the bran cereal to soften.

6 Next, you will add the dry ingredients on top of the wet ingredients and gently fold everything together until just combined, using a rubber spatula. Be certain not to overwork the batter or your muffins will get tough.

7 Scoop your batter with a large spoon or ice cream scoop into muffin tins, filling it just to the top, then bake for 15-20 minutes—you'll know they're ready when a toothpick tester comes out with just a few moist crumbs attached.

8 While the muffins are baking, mix the granulated sugar and cinnamon for the topping and set aside.

9 As soon as you take them out of the oven, dust the tops of the muffins with the cinnamon-sugar mixture. As the muffins cool, this will create a nice, crunchy finish on top. Serve them as a healthy choice for a delicious breakfast treat. Enjoy!

 prep time: 20 minutes

 bake time: 15-20 minutes

 makes 12 muffins

what you'll need

muffins:
1½ cups all-purpose flour
2 tsp baking soda
1 tsp ground cinnamon (optional)
1 large egg
1 egg yolk
½ tsp kosher salt
⅔ cup brown sugar, firmly packed
3 Tbsp molasses
1 tsp pure vanilla extract
4 Tbsp unsalted butter, melted and cooled
¼ cup applesauce
1¾ cups plain whole milk yogurt
1¼ cups All Bran Original Cereal, left whole
1 cup All Bran Original Cereal, finely ground

topping:
2 Tbsp granulated sugar
½ tsp ground cinnamon (optional)

helpful hints

Don't have a food processor? A blender will work just as well to produce finely ground cereal.

If you don't have molasses on hand, you can always substitute dark corn syrup, agave or honey.

CINNAMON SUGAR MONKEY BREAD

let's do it

1 To make the bread, pour lukewarm water into the mixing bowl of a stand mixer fitted with a dough hook. Stir in yeast and ½ tsp sugar. Set aside and allow the yeast to activate in the sugar water for 10 minutes—you'll know you've activated the yeast if the mixture becomes foamy. If it doesn't, your water may be too hot or too cold and you'll need to start over!

2 Microwave milk, butter and salt in a small bowl for about 1 minute then set aside to cool. Crack eggs into a 1 cup liquid measuring cup then add water until the measurement reaches ½ cup then set aside.

3 Add 2 cups flour and ½ cup sugar to the yeast mixture. Mix on low until the flour is combined, then slowly add the egg and milk mixtures.

4 Add the remaining flour ½ cup at a time until dough forms and starts to pull away from the sides of the bowl then increase mixer setting to medium for about 5 minutes, until the dough is smooth and elastic.

5 Remove dough from the mixing bowl and form 18 balls that are slightly larger than a golf ball. (You'll only use half of the dough to make this recipe.)

6 Preheat the oven to 350 degrees and spray a Bundt pan with cooking spray.

7 Combine ¼ cup sugar and ½ tsp cinnamon in a resealable bag. Add the dough balls, 3 at a time, shake to coat then arrange evenly in the bottom of the pan.

8 Sprinkle the remaining cinnamon sugar over the balls then cover the pan loosely with foil and allow the dough to rise in a warm spot for about 1 hour.

9 Microwave the brown sugar, butter, cinnamon and salt together in a small bowl until melted. Stir to combine then pour over dough. Place the pan on a baking sheet and bake for 25 minutes or until golden brown.

10 Remove from oven and cool 10 minutes before inverting onto a serving platter.

 prep time: 15 minutes

 bake time: 25 minutes

 makes 8-10 servings

what you'll need

bread:
1 package active dry yeast
¼ cup lukewarm water
   (100-115 degrees)
½ tsp granulated sugar
1 cup whole milk
5 Tbsp unsalted butter, room
   temperature
1 tsp kosher salt
2 large eggs, room temperature
4 ½ cups all-purpose flour, divided
½ cup granulated sugar

sugar coating:
¼ cup granulated sugar
½ tsp ground cinnamon

glaze:
¾ cup brown sugar, firmly packed
1 tsp ground cinnamon
6 Tbsp unsalted butter
½ tsp salt

helpful hint

Save time by using frozen yeast rolls from the grocery store. Defrost them according to directions on the package and begin the recipe from there.

CRUNCHY FRENCH TOAST

I don't know about you, but I find ordinary French toast boring. I coat challah or brioche bread with crushed cornflakes to add a crunchy texture. This meal is quick and easy to make and my kids love it!

let's do it

1 Slice the bread into 1" thick slices and allow it to sit uncovered to dry out just a bit—you can actually allow the bread to sit out for several hours if needed.

2 Place the crushed cornflakes on a plate and reserve.

3 Whisk the eggs, milk, vanilla, cinnamon and salt in a medium-sized bowl until they are completely blended.

4 Dip 1 slice of bread into the milk mixture for just a brief moment, turn to coat the opposite side of the bread, then immediately dredge the bread in the crushed cornflakes. Press lightly to make sure the cornflakes adhere to the bread then place the slice on a baking sheet lined with wax paper. Repeat with your remaining slices of bread.

5 You're now ready to cook the French toast! Melt approximately 1 Tbsp of unsalted butter in a large non-stick skillet over medium heat. Add as many slices of French toast to the skillet as it will comfortably hold and cook 3-4 minutes on each side until the slices are golden brown and crispy on each side. Wipe the skillet clean between batches then add an additional Tbsp of butter to the skillet. Start the next batch and repeat the process until all of the French toast slices are cooked.

6 French toast can be kept warm for up to 1 hour in the oven. Just cover the cooked slices of French toast and place in an oven set at 200 degrees.

7 Dust the French toast with powdered sugar and drizzle with plenty of warm maple syrup. Serve and enjoy!

 prep time: 15 minutes

 cook time: 6-8 minutes

 makes 8-10 servings

what you'll need

1 loaf challah or brioche bread
2 cups cornflake cereal, crushed
2 large eggs
¾ cup whole milk
1 tsp pure vanilla extract
1 tsp ground cinnamon
¼ tsp salt
2-3 Tbsp unsalted butter
¼ cup powdered sugar
maple syrup

helpful hints

Challah or brioche breads are light, buttery egg breads that are perfect for French toast. Try raisin or cinnamon swirl for a variation.

One of the best skills you can learn as a cook is how to manage heat. This recipe is a great example of the importance of that, because if the heat is too high, the outside will be crispy before the interior has had a chance to cook/set.

PEGGY'S BANANA BREAD

This recipe is also great for banana nut muffins. Use the same oven temp but bake only 18-20 minutes. You'll have individual servings of this moist, yummy bread set to go for breakfast or a snack!

let's do it

1 Preheat the oven to 350 degrees and butter and flour 2 standard-sized loaf pans. I rub the wrapper from the cube of butter inside the loaf pans—there's usually just enough butter left to lightly grease the pans. Then I add 1 Tbsp of flour and knock it around until it covers the pan.

2 Sift the flour, baking soda and salt into a small bowl then set aside.

3 Cream together butter or oil and sugar until light and fluffy. Add the eggs and beat until completely incorporated, scraping down the sides of the bowl if necessary. Stir in the buttermilk and mashed bananas just until combined.

4 Add the flour mixture to the wet ingredients and fold gently until all of the flour is incorporated. Don't wash out that bowl yet! Place the nuts into the bowl, toss them with the teaspoon of additional flour and make sure each nut is completely dusted with flour before adding it to the batter so they don't sink to the bottom. Fold the nuts into the batter to distribute them evenly.

5 Divide the batter evenly between the 2 prepared loaf pans. Set both pans on a baking sheet to catch anything that might flow over. Plus, it makes it much easier to maneuver the pans in and out of the oven.

6 Bake the loaves for about 1 hour or until a toothpick comes out clean and the center of each loaf is firm to the touch.

7 Cover the loaves with a lint-free kitchen towel and set them on a rack until they're cool enough to handle. Remove the banana bread from the loaf pans, slice and serve while it's nice and warm!

 prep time: 15 minutes

 bake time: 60 minutes

 makes 2 loaves

what you'll need

3 cups all-purpose flour
1½ tsp baking soda
½ tsp salt
½ cup unsalted butter or vegetable oil
1½ cups granulated sugar
2 large eggs
½ cup plus 2 Tbsp buttermilk
3-4 very ripe bananas, mashed
½ cup chopped walnuts or pecans
1 tsp all-purpose flour

helpful hints

Place green bananas in a brown paper bag with an apple or tomato overnight to speed up the ripening process.

Lightly mash bananas, leaving a few pieces and chunks—don't turn them into a fine puree. Mashing bananas too much will leave a gummy layer on the bottom of your bread.

OVERNIGHT BREAKFAST CASSEROLE

I love anything that I can make ahead of time, and this recipe actually requires it! Add sausage, bacon or veggies for an extra-hearty breakfast that's ready to pop in the oven when you wake up!

let's do it

1 Place a skillet over medium-high heat and cook sausage until it's cooked all the way through. Then transfer the cooked sausage to a paper towel-lined plate to drain while you prepare the rest of the casserole.

2 Tear the sourdough bread into 1" chunks then place them into a greased 10" square baking dish. Sprinkle the cooked sausage and cheddar cheese over the bread.

3 In a medium bowl, beat the eggs for several minutes before adding the milk, salt, pepper and paprika. Make sure the spices are well distributed throughout the egg. Pour the egg mixture over the ingredients in the baking dish and cover with foil. Refrigerate overnight while you relax and get a good night's sleep.

4 The next morning, preheat the oven to 350 degrees and remove the casserole from the fridge.

5 Bake uncovered for 20-30 minutes until the casserole is heated through and the eggs are set. You won't have to say, "Breakfast is ready!" more than once!

 prep time: 20 minutes

 bake time: 15-20 minutes

 makes 6-8 servings

what you'll need

1 lb ground breakfast sausage
5 thick slices of sourdough bread
2 cups shredded cheddar cheese
8 large eggs, well beaten
2 ½ cups milk
¼ tsp salt
½ tsp pepper
½ tsp paprika

helpful hints

The secret to this recipe is whisking the eggs for 2-3 minutes. Incorporating air into them will cause the combined ingredients to rise, creating a lighter, fluffier casserole.

Don't like sausage? Substitute bacon. For crispy bacon, make sure it's room temperature and spaced evenly on a cold skillet before cooking over medium-low heat.

MAIN MEALS

The bulk of this book is main dishes for a reason; I am constantly on the prowl for new ideas for dinner. I get tired of the same ole chicken dinners and need inspiration to mix things up a bit. However, I wanted to stay true to classic suppers. You won't find obscure flavor combinations or terms you've never heard of in this cookbook. These meals are dependable recipes for everyday family meals!

I have developed these recipes based on what I grew up eating and loving, recipes I feel could use a little updating for the modern palate without changing them so drastically that you no longer recognize them. My mom had to go in for heart surgery right before Thanksgiving this year so she wasn't able to do all her normal holiday cooking. The first thing my daughter said to me when she found out I was cooking most of our Thanksgiving meal was: "Please, Mommy, don't change Grandma's noodles!" So, you'll also find a few family recipes that I wouldn't dare touch! These recipes haven't stood the test of time for nothing!! They are so, so yummy. I can't wait to hear what you think of them.

opposite page: My family on Christmas Eve–Mama, Peggy; Daddy, Jack; sister, Jackie; and I'm in the glasses and corduroy jumpsuit. Family favorite: pork chops with mushroom gravy.

Pork Chops

4 tablespoon butter
4 pork chops
1/2 cup wine
1 teaspoon salt
1/8 pepper
1/2 teaspoon crushed dried rosemary
2 cloves garlic minced
1/2 onion
mushrooms sliced

1. In large skillet, melt butter over med heat. Cook chops in butter, turning once to brown evenly. Remove from pan - cook onions in juice + butter in pan. Pour in wine & season salt, pepper, rosemary + garlic Add chops back in skillet Simmer, uncovered for 20 minutes or until chop are tender. Transfer to plate & spoon sauce over the meat

HOT TURKEY PASTRAMI SANDWICHES

My hot turkey pastrami sandwiches are a family favorite not just because we can eat on the go—but also because there's no fuss and zero dirty dishes. It makes me wonder why I don't cook like this all the time!

let's do it

1 Set the rack in the center of the oven then preheat to 375 degrees. Meanwhile, slice the buns in half—but don't cut them all the way through. You'll want to leave a small amount attached on one side to help hold your ingredients within the bun.

2 Spread mustard on both sides of the bun then pile on the pastrami and turkey. Add the sliced cheese then wrap each sandwich in an individual sheet of aluminum foil.

3 Place the sandwiches on a baking sheet then bake for 10-12 minutes—until the centers of your sandwiches are nice and warm.

4 Remove sandwiches from oven then serve immediately. If you're transporting them to a picnic or potluck or eating on the go, place the sandwiches in an insulated bag, then vamoose!

 prep time: 10 minutes

 bake time: 10 minutes

makes 8 sandwiches

what you'll need

8 sesame seed buns
4 Tbsp yellow mustard
1 lb pastrami, thinly sliced
1 lb turkey, thinly sliced
8 slices smoked Gouda cheese
aluminum foil sheets

helpful hints

Avoid baking your sandwiches with condiments like tomatoes or lettuce—they will make the buns soggy. Add the condiments last if you can't live without 'em!

When making this recipe, slice the bun, leaving a small portion connected at the bottom—this will keep your ingredients intact when you bite into the sandwich!

MEATLOAF SLIDERS

I would bet almost every American kid had meatloaf growing up. I update this nostalgic crowd-pleaser and crank it up a notch with salsa and jalapeños.

let's do it

1 Preheat the oven to 350 degrees then coat a baking sheet with cooking spray and set it aside.

2 Mix all ingredients (except the buns, of course) in a medium-sized bowl until completely combined.

3 Divide the mixture into 6 equal portions, roll each portion into a ball then place each of them on the baking sheet. Press the balls flat using the bottom of a glass.

4 Place the baking sheet on the center rack of the oven and bake the patties for 25 minutes. Allow the patties to rest at room temperature for 5 minutes before placing them on the buns. Garnish your sliders with any of your favorite toppings and enjoy!

 prep time: 15 minutes

 bake time: 25 minutes

 makes 6 sliders

what you'll need

½ cup plain breadcrumbs
2 large eggs, beaten
½ cup shredded Mexican cheese blend
1 lb lean ground beef
¼ cup fresh salsa
¼ cup red onion, finely diced
1 jalapeño, minced
1 Tbsp garlic, minced
1 tsp chili powder
1 tsp ground cumin
salt and black pepper, to taste
6 egg slider buns

helpful hints

Jalapeños add an unexpected kick that may be too strong for the kids. You can always sauté them first for a couple of minutes to soften the flavor.

It's easy to flatten these sliders with the bottom of a glass. Dip the glass in water between each press to keep it from sticking to the meat.

CHICKEN SLOPPY JOES

I used ground chicken and a unique blend of ingredients for a subtle, Polynesian flavor for my sloppy joes recipe. It's a great dish for a party or potluck—double the batch and load up the slow cooker!

let's do it

1 Heat the oil in a large skillet over medium-high heat until it's shimmering. Add the onion and Anaheim pepper then cook for about 3 minutes, until the onion is translucent. Add garlic and chili powder then cook for 1 additional minute.

2 Add the ground chicken to the skillet and use a wooden spoon to break it into small pieces. Be careful not to overcook the chicken or it will become chewy as you continue to cook the sauce. Cook for approximately 3-4 minutes until the chicken is white with just a little pink throughout.

3 Add the salt, tomato sauce, dry mustard, crushed pineapple (including its juice) and the Worcestershire sauce. Stir to combine and bring the mixture to a bubble.

4 When the liquid begins to boil, immediately reduce the heat to medium-low and simmer for about 15 minutes or until the mixture has thickened to the proper "sloppy joe" consistency.

5 About 5 minutes before serving, toast and steam your buns. The key to a great bun is to toast it a little and steam it to make it super soft. Heat a well-seasoned cast iron skillet, open and butter the buns then place them open-faced, 2 at a time in the center of the pan. Take about 2 Tbsp of water and run it down the side of the skillet—it'll start to sizzle and create steam. Quickly cover the skillet and let the toasting and steaming commence!

6 Fill the warm toasted buns with a generous amount of the sloppy joe filling and wrap in aluminum foil to keep them warm. Serve to your hungry family or a crowd and enjoy!

 prep time: 10 minutes

 cook time: 30 minutes

 makes 8 sandwiches

what you'll need

2 Tbsp olive oil
1 yellow onion, finely diced
1 Anaheim pepper (or ½ green bell pepper), finely diced
3 cloves garlic, minced
1 tsp chili powder
2 lbs ground chicken
1 tsp salt
15 oz can tomato sauce
½ tsp dry mustard
1 cup crushed pineapple (do not drain)
2 Tbsp Worcestershire sauce
8 sesame seed hamburger buns
2 Tbsp unsalted butter, softened

helpful hints

If you don't have or can't find ground chicken, cut chicken breasts into 1" chunks and pulse in a food processor until it's finely ground but not a paste.

You want the sauce to reduce down and thicken so that it doesn't wet the bun when you assemble the sandwiches.

CHICKEN ENCHILADA SOUP

Get the rich flavor you crave from your favorite Mexican dish! My chicken enchilada soup recipe is a fun and unique way to eat your enchiladas—it's thick and hearty!

let's do it

1 Add chicken broth and chicken breasts to a soup pot then bring to a boil over high heat. When the broth starts to boil, reduce the heat to low and allow ingredients to simmer for about 15-20 minutes until the chicken breasts are cooked through.

2 Remove the pot from the stove then transfer the chicken breasts onto a plate to cool. Strain the broth into a large bowl and reserve. Once the chicken is cool enough to handle, shred or cube it then set aside.

3 Adjust the heat to a medium setting then return the pot to the stove. Add canola oil, onions and garlic then cook for 3-4 minutes to soften the onions. Add the tomato purée, reserved chicken breast and chicken broth. Let the mixture come to a boil while you prepare the remaining ingredients.

4 Using the same bowl that the chicken broth was in, whisk together the corn meal, water, enchilada sauce, chili pepper and cumin until no lumps remain. Pour the mixture into the soup pot, whisking diligently.

5 Now that you've added most of the remaining ingredients, allow the soup to come to a boil with the heat still set to medium—the soup will thicken as the temperature of the mixture increases. You'll want to stir every 2-3 minutes to avoid scorching your soup until the liquid starts to bubble.

6 When the soup achieves a bubble, immediately reduce the heat to low then gradually begin adding the cheese. Stir constantly until it's completely melted and well incorporated into the soup.

7 Add salt to taste and serve garnished with shredded cheddar cheese, tortilla strips, avocado, cilantro and sour cream.

 prep time: 15 minutes

 cook time: 45 minutes

 makes 8-10 servings

what you'll need

2-3 boneless, skinless chicken breasts
49 oz can chicken broth
2 Tbsp canola oil
1 medium yellow onion, finely diced
2 cloves garlic, minced
14.5 oz can tomato purée
½ cup corn meal, finely ground
2 cups water
19 oz can mild red enchilada sauce
1 tsp chili powder
½ tsp cumin
16 oz block American cheese, diced small
salt to taste

helpful hints

Some like it hot! Adjust the heat level of the soup by choosing a hot, medium or mild red enchilada sauce.

If you own an immersion blender, it will come in handy with this recipe. Just puree the soup right in the pot to avoid extra dishes! If you're using a countertop blender, fill the pitcher 1/3 of the way to avoid overflow.

BLACK BEAN SOUP

let's do it

1 Pour the bag of black beans onto a rimmed baking sheet then give the pan a good shake to make a single layer of beans. Remove any stones, debris or unappealing beans and discard. Once the beans have been sorted, transfer them to a colander and rinse under cool water until the water runs clear.

2 Place the washed beans into a large pot then add the water, ½ yellow onion (quartered), ½ bunch of cilantro (stems and all), bay leaf, ham hock and salt—then bring to a boil over high heat. Once the pot achieves a rolling boil, reduce heat to low then skim any foam that rises to the top.

3 Once foam stops forming, cover and continue to cook on a low setting for approximately 2 hours, stirring every 20 minutes. When 2 hours have passed, remove the ham hock from the mixture and set it aside to cool.

4 Keep your pot of beans over low heat. Meanwhile, remove the good meat from the ham hock then discard the skin, fat and bones. Next, remove the bay leaves and cilantro (stems and all) and discard.

5 In a medium-sized skillet, sauté the finely diced onion, Anaheim pepper, garlic, chili powder, and cumin in 2 Tbsp olive oil over medium heat. Cook for about 3 minutes until the onions become transparent. Transfer the sauté mixture and 1 cup of the cooked beans (with a little bit of their liquid) into a blender or food processor then puree.

6 Add the puree back into the pot of beans then stir to combine. Cover the pot and allow the ingredients to simmer for an additional 30 minutes.

7 Stir in the lime juice and chopped cilantro then serve with accompaniments such as sour cream, chopped green onion, lime wedges, shredded cheese and tortilla chips. Enjoy!

 prep time: 30 minutes

 cook time: 2 1/2 hours

 makes 12-14 servings

what you'll need

1 lb black beans

10 cups water

½ yellow onion, quartered

½ bunch fresh cilantro

1 bay leaf

1 smoked ham hock (omit for vegetarian version)

1 Tbsp kosher salt

2 Tbsp olive oil

1 yellow onion, finely diced

1 Anaheim pepper, seeded and chopped

4-6 medium garlic cloves, pressed

1½ tsp chili powder

1 tsp cumin

juice from ½ of a lime

¼ bunch fresh cilantro leaves, chopped

helpful hints

You don't have to pre-soak the beans for this recipe, but you do need to sort the beans and check for rocks and debris. When beans are harvested then bagged, you'll often find tiny rocks in the mix.

Make certain the water level remains above the beans throughout the cooking process—add hot water as needed if the beans are not adequately submerged.

TEXAS CHILI

You know it's fall when you're inspired to whip up a big ole pot of chili. Feed your family and warm your soul with my hearty Texas chili recipe—this is one of my daddy's favorite meals!

let's do it

1 Heat olive oil in a large pot or Dutch oven over medium-high heat. Add the diced onion then cook about 3-4 minutes until it's translucent. Add the garlic then cook for about 5 more minutes, stirring frequently.

2 Add ground beef using a wooden spoon to break up the pieces—the chunks of beef should be about the size of a pea. Continue to cook the meat until it's completely browned then drain off the fat and return the pot to the stove.

3 Add tomato sauce, tomato juice, sugar, bay leaves and salt then bring to a boil. Reduce the heat to medium-low then add remaining seasonings, stirring until the ingredients are well incorporated.

4 Cover the pot and allow the chili to simmer for 45 minutes to 1 hour, stirring often.

5 Serve piping hot with shredded cheese and diced onion. Enjoy!

 prep time: 15 minutes

 cook time: 1-1½ hours

 makes 8-10 servings

what you'll need

2 Tbsp olive oil

1 yellow onion, finely diced

2 garlic cloves, minced

2 lbs ground beef

4 cups low-sodium tomato juice

8 oz can tomato sauce

pinch of granulated sugar

2 bay leaves

1½ tsp kosher salt

3 Tbsp chili powder

1 tsp paprika

½ tsp cumin

¼ tsp garlic powder

¼ tsp onion powder

helpful hints

Some meals taste better after they sit overnight and this dish is no exception! Prepare my Texas chili recipe a day or two in advance then store it, pot and all, in the fridge until you're ready to serve.

The secret to making this dish more flavorful is to break up the ground beef into super small pieces while it cooks.

CHICKEN STOCK

let's do it

1 Place large stock pot filled with cold water on stove without heat.

2 Fry bacon in a heavy bottom skillet on medium heat until crispy. Remove and reserve for later, keeping skillet with bacon drippings on medium heat.

3 Add olive oil to the skillet and allow it to heat for about 1 minute. Add chicken pieces and sauté for approximately 5 minutes on each side. Remove chicken from the skillet as they are cooked and add them to the pot of cold water.

4 Once all of the chicken pieces have been seared and added to the pot of water, add the carrots, onions, celery, thyme and bay leaves. Turn the heat to high, bring the liquid to a bubble and immediately reduce the heat to medium-low. Maintain the stock at a low simmer for approximately 30 minutes.

5 Once the stock has been simmering for 30 minutes, remove chicken and pull the meat from the bones but don't discard those chicken bones! Set aside to cool then place the chicken meat in a sealed container in the refrigerator for up to 3 days before adding to my rustic chicken soup recipe on page 48. Or save it for any dish requiring pulled chicken.

6 Return bones to the pot. Continue to slowly simmer the stock (uncovered) on low for 4 hours, skimming any foam that rises to the surface. Feel free to add only enough hot water to keep the chicken bones and vegetables covered while simmering—allowing a little bit of water to cook off will concentrate the flavor of your finished stock.

7 Once the stock has simmered a good 4-5 hours, strain the liquid through a fine mesh sieve lined with a bit of cheesecloth. Discard the bones and vegetables then skim the fat from the top of the stock and season with salt to taste.

 prep time: 20-25 minutes

 cook time: 5 hours

 makes 3 qts chicken stock

what you'll need

4 qts cold water

4 slices bacon

2 Tbsp olive oil

3-4 lbs chicken, cut into pieces

3 large carrots, peeled and cut into 2" pieces

½ medium yellow onion, quartered

4 stalks celery, cut into thirds

3 sprigs thyme

bay leaves

sea salt to taste

helpful hints

Always start with cold water, don't stir and never let your stock boil too fast or it will become cloudy. Always keep it on a light simmer, NOT a rolling boil.

If you are not going to use the stock immediately, allow it to cool on your countertop until you are able to place it in the fridge. Refrigerated stock will keep for 1 week and frozen stock will stay good for up to 6 months!

MAMA'S HOMEMADE NOODLES

Holiday dinners wouldn't be the same without my mama's noodles because nothing compares to homemade. Once you get the hang of how to make them, you'll use them for soups, stews or even serve them plain!

let's do it

1 Add 1 cup flour and the baking powder into a medium-sized mixing bowl and stir to distribute the baking powder evenly throughout the flour.

2 Beat the eggs, salt and milk in a small bowl. Pour the wet ingredients into the flour and baking powder then mix until combined—at this point the mixture will be quite wet.

3 Continue to add extra flour in small increments as needed to make the dough just firm enough to form into a ball. Cover the dough in plastic wrap and let it rest at room temperature for 30 minutes.

4 After the dough has rested for at least 30 minutes, roll it out onto a heavily floured board using a rolling pin. Dust the top of the dough with as much flour as needed to keep the rolling pin from sticking. Don't worry about how much flour you are adding—at this point you can't add too much. The noodles will take as much flour as they need and leave the rest on the board. Just be sure to keep enough flour on both sides of the dough to keep it from sticking. You want to roll the noodles quite thin because they will puff up when they are cooked.

5 After the dough has been thinly rolled out, let it rest on the counter for 1-2 hours, turning it over once so that it can dry a little bit on each side.

6 Cut the dough into thin, short strips using a pizza cutter and dust the noodles with a little bit more flour to keep them from sticking together. You can cook them right away for approximately 30 minutes, depending on how firm you like your noodles or refrigerate them until you are ready to use them. You can also freeze your noodles for up to 1 month if you have more than you can use. Enjoy!

 prep time: 20 minutes

 inactive prep time: 1-2 hours

 makes 10 servings

what you'll need

1-2 cups all-purpose flour
¼ tsp baking powder
3 large eggs, beaten
1 tsp salt
1 Tbsp milk

helpful hints

Don't be intimidated that this recipe leaves you somewhat to your own devices concerning the amount of flour. Use as much as you need to spread on your rolling surface and dust the top of the dough so your rolling pin rolls freely over the dough.

A pizza cutter is a handy tool for making quick work of cutting noodles.

TWO-DAY RUSTIC CHICKEN NOODLE SOUP

This perfect make-ahead recipe looks complicated but, if you have the time, it's easy to follow. I do the prepping in one day and assemble and cook the next. Homemade chicken stock and noodles make all the difference in this recipe.

let's do it

1 First, make the flavor base by mincing the onion, celery and garlic in a food processor.

2 Next, place a large soup pot over medium-high heat and melt the butter. Add in the minced veggies and fresh thyme then cook 1-2 minutes, being careful not to burn them.

3 Add the chicken broth and scrape the bottom of the pan to loosen anything that is sticking. Continue cooking until the liquid has reduced and only a paste remains.

4 Once the flavor base has cooked down into a paste, immediately add 3 qts of chicken stock, along with the baby carrots, chopped onion, sliced celery, reserved chicken meat and your choice of frozen veggies. Bring the liquid to a boil, reduce the heat to medium-low then simmer the soup for 45 minutes to 1 hour.

5 About 40 minutes before you are ready to serve the soup, increase the heat to medium and allow the soup to come to a bubble. Add noodles and return to a boil then reduce the heat once again and simmer for at least 30 minutes. Enjoy!

Day 1

make the homemade chicken stock on page 44
make the noodles on page 46

Day 2

make the soup!

what you'll need

½ medium yellow onion, quartered
2 celery stalks, cleaned, trimmed and
    cut into chunks
2 cloves of garlic, peeled
2 Tbsp unsalted butter
1 tsp fresh thyme
1 cup chicken broth
3 qts chicken stock (recipe on page 44)
½ lb baby carrots, or 3 large carrots,
    peeled and cut into 2" pieces
½ medium yellow onion, chopped
4 stalks celery, sliced
reserved chicken meat (from making
    the stock)
2 cups fresh or frozen green beans,
    cut into 2" pieces
mama's egg noodles (recipe page 46)
    or 12 oz package of egg noodles

helpful hints

If you like your vegetables firmer, then don't add them to the soup until it has already been cooking for about 20 minutes.

Keep an eye out when cooking garlic! It only takes a minute—if it burns you might as well start over!

TOMATO HOT DISH

My friend Molly inspired this recipe and it's been a family favorite for years! Add your favorite things like cooked spinach, ground beef, zucchini squash or cheese to make this dish your own.

let's do it

1 Set the rack to the center of the oven and preheat to 350 degrees. Spray an 8" x 8" casserole dish with cooking spray then set aside.

2 Parboil the pasta in plenty of salted, boiling water for about 3-4 minutes. Drain the pasta, rinse with cool water then set aside. Don't worry about undercooking pasta, as it will continue to cook in the sauce once placed in the oven. Just cook it long enough to release the starches.

3 Heat olive oil in a large skillet over medium heat then add the onion and cook for about 4-5 minutes until it's translucent. Add the garlic and cook an additional 2 minutes.

4 Blend the tomatoes in a food processor or blender to the desired consistency. Then add them to the skillet, along with the dried basil, dried oregano and salt. Heat until bubbly then reduce the heat to low and simmer for 5 minutes.

5 Once the sauce has had a chance to simmer, stir in fresh basil leaves and pasta. Stir to coat the pasta evenly with the sauce.

6 Transfer pasta to the prepared casserole dish, cover with aluminum foil then bake for 20 minutes. Remove the foil and bake an additional 5-10 minutes until the sauce is bubbly. Remove from the oven and cool 5 minutes before serving. Enjoy!

 prep time: 15 minutes

 bake time: 30 minutes

 makes 9 servings

what you'll need

8 oz rotini pasta

¼ cup extra virgin olive oil

1 medium yellow onion, finely diced

2 cloves garlic, minced

28 oz can San Marzano tomatoes, pureed or chopped to desired consistency

½ tsp dried oregano

1 tsp dried basil

½ tsp sea salt or kosher salt

½ tsp granulated sugar

6-8 fresh basil leaves, torn

helpful hints

No need to add oil when cooking pasta! Lower the heat slightly and stir often to keep it from sticking together and foaming.

A San Marzano tomato is a thicker-skinned variation of a Roma tomato. Originating in volcanic soil near Mount Vesuvius, it's slightly sweeter and less acidic. If using canned tomatoes, add extra sugar to adjust the acidity.

SWEET LASAGNA

This lasagna freezes so well you'll want to make an extra batch! Frozen lasagna is my go-to dish for dinner on the fly.

let's do it

1 Place a rack in the center of the oven and preheat to 350 degrees. Spray a 9" x 13" casserole with cooking spray and set it aside.

2 For the meat sauce, set a large pot over medium-high heat and brown the ground beef with onion, garlic, salt and pepper. When the beef has cooked through, drain the fat and return to medium-high heat. Stir in whole tomatoes, tomato sauce, parsley, basil and sugar, breaking up the tomatoes as the sauce heats. Bring sauce to a boil, immediately reduce the heat to low then simmer for 45 minutes or until thickened.

3 While the meat mixture simmers, parboil the lasagna noodles, cooking them for only 3-4 minutes, then drain and set aside.

4 In a medium mixing bowl, stir together the cottage cheese, ¼ cup of Parmesan, parsley and oregano. Set aside until you are ready to assemble the lasagna.

5 Begin assembling the lasagna by spreading 1 cup of meat sauce in the bottom of the casserole dish then layer with 4 lasagna noodles. Spread ⅓ of the cheese mixture on top of the noodles (this will be very thick and will not cover the entire dish—drop by the spoonful onto noodles and lightly spread). Spread another cup of meat sauce over the cheese layer then sprinkle lightly with mozzarella cheese.

6 Repeat layers, finishing with the last of the noodles topped with remaining meat sauce and mozzarella cheese. Sprinkle Parmesan cheese on top and cover casserole dish with aluminum foil.

7 Place lasagna in the oven and bake for 30 minutes. Then remove the foil and bake an additional 15 minutes. Remove from oven and allow to cool for at least 15 minutes before cutting. Serve and wait for the rave reviews!

 prep time: 1 hour

 bake time: 45 minutes

 makes one 9" x 13" lasagna

what you'll need

2 lb ground sirloin

½ tsp salt

½ tsp pepper

1 medium yellow onion, diced small

1 clove garlic, minced

14.5 oz can whole tomatoes

15 oz can tomato sauce

2 Tbsp fresh parsley, chopped

2 tsp dried basil

1 Tbsp granulated sugar

16 lasagna noodles

16 oz container small curd cottage cheese, drained

¼ cup grated Parmesan cheese

1 Tbsp parsley, chopped

1½ tsp dried oregano

16 oz bag shredded mozzarella cheese

¼ cup grated Parmesan cheese (for topping)

helpful hint

To be sure your lasagna sets up nicely, cook meat sauce till it's no longer runny, pour off any standing liquid from the cottage cheese and drain the lasagna noodles well.

OLD-FASHIONED MAC 'N' CHEESE

My favorite mac 'n' cheese recipe combines cheddar with the sweet, nutty flavor of Gruyere cheese. The trick to a smooth sauce is to constantly stir it, so don't walk away while making this dish!

let's do it

1 Preheat the oven to 350 degrees, spray a 9" x 13" casserole dish with cooking spray and set it aside.

2 Place a large pot of water on the stove, add a pinch of salt and bring to a boil. Add the elbow macaroni and cook for 3 minutes, until the noodles are soft but still firm. Drain in a colander, rinse under cool water to stop it from cooking then set aside.

3 Next, return your pot to the stove and melt the butter over medium heat. Once the butter has melted, sprinkle evenly with flour using a whisk to combine. Continue stirring for about 1 minute then add salt and mustard and cook another 2 minutes.

4 Slowly whisk in milk and allow the mixture to come to a bubble, stirring constantly. Reduce the heat to low and simmer for 3 minutes. Be sure to stir the sauce constantly so it doesn't scorch on the bottom! The consistency will be similar to a thin pancake batter.

5 Once the sauce has simmered for 3 minutes, add the cheddar and Gruyere cheeses ½ cup at a time. The heat should remain on low. Be certain to completely melt each addition of cheese before adding the next. When all of the cheese has been added and has melted completely, add the macaroni and stir to combine.

6 Transfer the macaroni and cheese to the prepared 9" x 13" casserole dish. (You may want to place the dish on a baking sheet in case the sauce spills over.) Sprinkle breadcrumbs on top if desired and dust with paprika to add a little color.

7 Bake uncovered 20-25 minutes for a creamy texture, or 30-35 minutes for a crispy toasted top. Serve and enjoy!

 prep time: 30 minutes

 cook time: 25-40 minutes

 makes one 9" x 13" casserole

what you'll need

1 box elbow macaroni
4 Tbsp unsalted butter
¼ cup all-purpose flour
2 tsp salt
½ tsp dry mustard
2 ¾ cups whole milk
2 cups mild cheddar cheese, grated
1 cup Gruyere cheese, grated
¾ cup breadcrumbs for topping
    (optional)
paprika (for dusting)

helpful hints

Gruyere is a high-grade Swiss cheese. If you're looking for a good alternative, use Monterey Jack but don't use American Swiss cheese because it's way too dry.

COTTAGE PIE

let's do it

1 Preheat the oven to 375 degrees and spray a 9" deep pie dish with cooking spray.

2 Place potatoes into a medium saucepan with enough cold water to cover them by at least 1". Bring to a boil over high heat, reduce heat to medium-low then simmer until potatoes are fork tender.

3 Drain potatoes and place them in a medium-sized bowl. Add butter, sour cream, salt and onion powder and whip until light and fluffy. Cover and set aside.

4 Add ground beef, onions and carrots to a large skillet over medium-high heat. Break the ground beef into pieces and continue cooking until no pink remains. Add garlic and cook an additional minute then drain off the fat.

5 Return skillet to the stove and reduce heat to medium. Sprinkle meat with flour and stir until combined. Cook 1 minute before stirring in beef broth, tomato paste, Worcestershire sauce and rosemary. Bring the mixture to a boil then immediately reduce heat to low and simmer for 5-6 minutes until filling has thickened.

6 Remove filling from the heat and stir in frozen peas. Transfer filling into the prepared pie dish, then spread reserved mashed potatoes over the top of the beef mixture—make sure to spread the potatoes all the way to the edges to seal filling inside.

7 Brush potato topping lightly with the beaten egg and place pie dish on a rimmed baking sheet in case it bubbles over. Bake 25-30 minutes or until tips of potatoes turn golden brown and filling is nice and bubbly. Cool 10 minutes before serving. Enjoy!

 prep time: 20 minutes

 bake time: 25 minutes

 makes one 9" deep-dish cottage pie

what you'll need

topping:
2 large Russet potatoes,
  peeled and cubed
2 Tbsp unsalted butter
¼ cup sour cream
½ tsp salt
¼ tsp onion powder

filling:
1 lb lean ground beef
½ medium yellow onion, finely diced
2 medium carrots, finely diced
1 clove garlic, minced
2 Tbsp all-purpose flour
1¼ cup beef broth or beef consommé
1 tsp tomato paste
1 tsp Worcestershire sauce
1 tsp fresh rosemary, chopped finely
1 cup frozen peas
1 egg, well-beaten (for egg wash)

helpful hints

If you want to have more free time on the day you serve this recipe, make both the filling and topping in advance. Store them separately in the fridge then assemble and bake when you're ready for dinner.

If your potatoes are too thick, add a small amount of milk or additional sour cream to achieve the desired consistency.

CHEESEBURGER PIE

Cheeseburger pie is a delicious alternative to the ordinary burger in a bun—the CherylStyle team gave it a thumbs-up and so did my kiddos! With a little prep, it's oven-ready whenever you are.

let's do it

1 Preheat the oven to 375 degrees then spray your pie dish with cooking spray.

2 Place the diced bacon into a medium-sized skillet set over medium-high heat and cook for about 6-7 minutes until crispy. Remove the bacon and place on a paper towel-lined plate and set aside.

3 Drain all but 2 Tbsp of bacon grease from the skillet, return the pan to medium-high heat and add ground beef. Break the beef into small pieces and cook for about 4 or 5 minutes until no pink remains. Add diced onion and beef bouillon, cook an additional 2-3 minutes then drain well. Once drained, transfer the beef mixture to the pie dish.

4 Next, add 1 cup of shredded cheese, the chopped tomatoes and bacon pieces to the beef mixture in your pie dish—make sure to reserve the remaining cup of shredded cheese for the topping. Smooth the mixture into an even layer then set aside.

5 Pour milk into a medium-sized mixing bowl and begin whisking. Slowly sprinkle in flour while whisking constantly—this will help to avoid any lumps. Add onion powder, salt and beaten eggs, whisking thoroughly until combined. Pour the milk mixture over the beef and jiggle the pan a bit to allow everything to combine.

6 Bake 25-30 minutes until the top is nicely browned and the center is set and firm to the touch. Top the pie with the remaining cup of cheese and return to the oven for an additional 3-5 minutes—just long enough to melt the cheese. Remove the pie from the oven, allow it to cool about 10 minutes then serve with all your favorite cheeseburger toppings. Enjoy!

 prep time: 30 minutes

 bake time: 30 minutes

 makes one 8" deep-dish pie

what you'll need

1 lb lean ground beef

8 oz thick cut bacon, diced

½ yellow onion, diced

1 tsp beef bouillon (2 small beef bouillon cubes)

2 cups shredded sharp cheddar cheese

2 Roma tomatoes, diced

1 cup milk

½ cup all-purpose flour

½ tsp onion powder

¼ tsp salt

2 large eggs, slightly beaten

helpful hints

Beef bouillon bumps up the flavor of this dish. If you don't have any on hand, you can substitute it with an equal amount of salt.

I line my colander with paper towels to get that extra bit of grease off of the cooked beef.

STUFFED CABBAGE CASSEROLE

Nothing says home cookin' like a savory, hearty and delicious casserole. My stuffed cabbage casserole recipe was derived from my love of traditional stuffed cabbage rolls, but this recipe is much easier to prepare!

 prep time: 30 minutes

 bake time: 75-90 minutes

 makes 12 servings

let's do it

1 Set the rack in the center of the oven then preheat to 350 degrees. Grease or spray a 9" x 13" casserole dish then set aside.

2 Cut the head of cabbage in half lengthwise then remove the core. Dice the leaves into ½" pieces then rinse in a colander and set aside.

3 Place ground beef in a large skillet and brown it completely over medium-high heat. Once the beef is cooked, remove the pan from the heat and drain excess grease.

4 Return the skillet to the cooktop then reduce the heat to medium-low. Add the onion, salt, pepper, paprika and oregano then cook for about 3-4 minutes until the onion is translucent.

5 Add the garlic and cabbage then cook the mixture for an additional 2 minutes, stirring well to combine the ingredients.

6 Remove the pan from heat, stir in the rice then transfer to a casserole dish and set aside. In a separate bowl, mix together the chicken broth and tomato sauce then pour the liquid over the cabbage mixture. Stir ingredients to combine evenly.

7 Cover the casserole dish with aluminum foil and seal it tightly. Bake for 75-90 minutes, stirring the casserole every 30 minutes and re-sealing the foil tightly each time. You'll know the casserole is done when the rice is cooked and the liquid has been absorbed.

8 Remove the casserole dish from the oven then allow it to rest for 10 minutes before serving. Enjoy!

what you'll need

1 lb ground beef
½ yellow onion, diced
½ tsp salt
¼ tsp pepper
½ tsp paprika
½ tsp dry oregano
3 cloves garlic, minced
1 head savoy cabbage, outer leaves removed, cored and diced into ½" pieces (approximately 8 cups chopped cabbage)
1 cup uncooked white rice
2½ cups beef or chicken broth
2 – 8 oz cans tomato sauce

helpful hints

A heavy earthenware or ceramic casserole dish is worth the investment! They heat evenly, prevent food from scorching and retain heat—they're practically indestructible!

You'll know the casserole is done when the rice has cooked completely and the liquid has been absorbed. If the casserole seems dry, simply heat a little water or broth then add it to the dish!

SHRIMP SCAMPI

let's do it

1 Bring a pot of salted water to a rolling boil over high heat. Add linguine and cook to al dente, according to package directions.

2 Meanwhile, sprinkle raw shrimp with 1 tsp kosher salt in a medium-sized bowl then stir to coat evenly. Allow shrimp to sit for 10 minutes. This process helps to extract water and make the texture of the shrimp firmer.

3 Rinse shrimp under cool water then pat dry with paper towels. When pasta is al dente, drain it in a colander then set aside until it's time to combine linguine with the sauce.

4 Heat olive oil in a large skillet over medium heat, swirling the oil to coat the bottom of pan. When the oil begins to shimmer, add shrimp, one at a time. Cook about 1 minute per side—until they're pink on both sides. The timing is important—you don't want to overcook the shrimp because you'll add them to the pan again later. Place the shrimp onto a plate and set aside.

5 Add butter, garlic and red pepper flakes to pan with heat still set to medium. Stir ingredients for 2-3 minutes until garlic softens. Add wine and lemon juice, stirring continuously, until liquid is reduced by half. You'll want to scrape the bottom and edges of the pan to ensure all of the yummy bits are incorporated into the mixture.

6 Return shrimp to skillet and add lemon slices. Stir mixture to evenly coat shrimp with lemon butter. Reduce heat to medium-low then cook until shrimp are firm and just cooked through. Test doneness of shrimp by cutting one in half—if the meat is opaque, the shrimp are done. Add pasta to the skillet and toss to combine. Sprinkle entire dish with fresh chopped parsley and serve!

 prep time: 30 minutes

 cook time: 20 minutes

 makes 6 servings

what you'll need

1 lb linguini pasta, cooked al dente

1 lb medium-sized shrimp, peeled and deveined

1 tsp kosher salt

¼ cup extra virgin olive oil

4 Tbsp unsalted butter

2 cloves garlic, chopped

1-2 pinches red pepper flakes

¼ cup dry white wine

½ cup fresh lemon juice (2-3 juicy lemons)

1 lemon, cut into slices

salt and fresh cracked black pepper

4 sprigs parsley, chopped

helpful hint

Despite claims that fresher is better, frozen shrimp is perfect for this recipe. Buying frozen shrimp not only saves you from having to peel and devein the little devils, but you also won't be on a timeline to make this recipe. Just throw the bag in the freezer until you're ready to cook.

INDIVIDUAL CHICKEN POT PIES

When serving this beloved dish to my kiddos, there's always a fight over the "good stuff" on top. To ensure everyone gets his or her fair share, I make individual pies—the dough is easier to handle too!

 prep time: 1 hour

 bake time: 35-40 minutes

 makes 4 individual pot pies

let's do it

1 To make pie crust, sift flour, sugar and salt together into a medium-sized bowl then stir to combine. Add oil and water then mix until dough forms a ball. Wrap dough in plastic wrap and allow it to rest 5-10 minutes in the fridge.

2 Remove chilled dough from fridge and roll it out between 2 sheets of wax paper until it's about ⅛" thick. Remove the top piece of wax paper and cut crust slightly larger than the diameter of ramekins to create an overlap. Transfer waxed paper to a baking sheet then refrigerate until ready to assemble.

3 To make the filling, melt butter in a large skillet over medium-high heat then add the chicken and onion. Cook 3-4 minutes until onions are translucent and chicken has turned white on all sides. Sprinkle flour, stir until it's absorbed into the butter and cook about 3 minutes, stirring constantly.

4 Add chicken broth, whisk until all lumps of flour are dissolved then stir in milk, poultry seasoning, garlic powder, salt and pepper. Bring mixture to a bubble, reduce heat to medium-low and cook 10-12 minutes until mixture has thickened. Remove from heat then fold in frozen veggies and set aside.

5 Preheat the oven to 425 degrees. Spray ramekins with cooking spray and remove crusts from fridge. Pour the filling into ramekins and brush egg wash around the outer edges of the ramekins to act as a glue to adhere the crust. Lay each crust on top of the filling and press the edges into the side of each dish to seal.

6 Poke a few holes in the top of the crust to allow steam to escape. Brush entire surface of crust with egg wash and sprinkle with coarse salt and pepper. Place ramekins on a baking sheet and bake 35-40 minutes. Remove the pies from the oven and wait 10 minutes before serving. Yum!

what you'll need

mama's pie crust:

2 cups all-purpose flour

pinch sugar

½ tsp salt

½ cup vegetable oil

¼ cup cold water

1 large egg, beaten with 1 Tbsp water (for egg wash)

filling:

4 Tbsp unsalted butter

3 - 6 oz boneless, skinless chicken breasts, cut into ½" cubes

½ yellow onion, finely diced

6 Tbsp all-purpose flour

2 cups low-sodium chicken broth

¾ cup milk

½ tsp poultry seasoning

¼ tsp garlic powder

½ tsp salt

¼ tsp pepper

12 oz frozen mixed vegetables (my kiddos love green beans, peas and carrots)

helpful hint

Using oil for this crust is an absolute must. It looks oilier than a butter-based crust but it's so delicious and easy you'll never make it any other way. Use this crust for your favorite pies.

ENCHILADA CHICKEN BAKE

Rather than chopping up chicken and rolling individual enchiladas, I marinate and dredge boneless, skinless chicken breasts in crushed tortilla chips. This recipe gives you a hearty portion of chicken to enjoy. It's great if you are trying to get more protein in your diet.

let's do it

1 Rinse the chicken breasts in cool water and pat them dry with a paper towel. In a large bowl, mix buttermilk, lemon juice, salsa or hot sauce, poultry seasoning, pepper and salt together until the ingredients are well combined.

2 Add the chicken breasts, making sure to submerge each breast in the buttermilk mixture. Cover the bowl with plastic wrap then allow the chicken to marinate in the fridge for at least 3 hours.

3 When you are ready to prepare the dish, preheat the oven to 350 degrees and spray a 13" x 9" baking dish with cooking spray.

4 Mix the crushed tortilla chips, garlic powder, paprika and parsley in a large bowl then set aside.

5 Remove breasts from the marinade and allow the excess buttermilk to drain away but leave any that remains clinging to the chicken. Dredge each breast in the tortilla chip mixture, pressing lightly to make sure they are thoroughly coated. Place the chicken in the baking dish and bake 30 minutes.

6 While the chicken is baking, heat the enchilada sauce in a saucepan over low to medium heat or use the microwave. You'll want your sauce to be nice and hot when you add it to the chicken.

7 Remove the chicken from the oven, pour the hot enchilada sauce over it and top with shredded cheeses. Return the chicken to the oven and bake an additional 15 minutes or until the chicken reaches an internal temperature of 165 degrees.

8 Garnish with sliced green onions and serve this dish while piping hot and bubbly.

 prep time: 30 minutes

 inactive prep time:
3 hours-overnight

 bake time: 45 minutes

 makes 4-6 servings

what you'll need

4 - 6 oz boneless, skinless chicken breasts
2 cups low-fat buttermilk
2 Tbsp lemon juice
¼ cups salsa or 2 Tbsp hot sauce
½ tsp poultry seasoning
1 tsp black pepper
2 tsp salt
5 cups tortilla chips, crushed
1 tsp garlic powder
½ tsp paprika
1 Tbsp fresh chopped parsley
19 oz can red enchilada sauce
1 cup shredded cheddar cheese
1 cup shredded Monterey Jack cheese
sliced green onions for garnish

helpful hints

If you like a spicier dish, try sprinkling cayenne pepper over your breaded chicken before you add the sauce.

If you don't have a food processor, crush chips in a plastic bag by beating with a wooden spoon until they're the size of breadcrumbs.

MEXICAN SKILLET CHICKEN

I love this dish served over fresh steamed rice but it can also be used as filling for chicken tacos. I make the consistency thicker then wrap it in warm tortillas and serve them with guacamole.

let's do it

1 First, add olive oil to a large sauté pan then place over medium-high heat. Add the diced chicken and cook about 3-4 minutes until all sides have turned white.

2 Add peppers, tomatoes, onions and garlic. Sauté on medium heat about 5-7 minutes until the onions are transparent.

3 Stir in broth, tomato paste, oregano, salt and pepper then bring to a boil.

4 Next, scatter the cilantro stems over the top of the chicken mixture (you can omit them if you prefer but you'll definitely be missing out on some flavor). Cover the skillet, reduce heat to medium-low then simmer for 30 minutes, stirring occasionally.

5 If you prefer the dish to have a thicker consistency, remove the lid for the last few minutes of cooking and allow some of the moisture to evaporate.

6 Remove the cilantro stems with a pair of tongs before serving. Spoon over white rice and enjoy!

 prep time: 15 minutes

 cook time: 40 minutes

 makes 8 servings

what you'll need

3 lbs boneless, skinless chicken
   breasts, cut into ½" cubes
2 Tbsp olive oil
2 Anaheim peppers or one green bell
   pepper, diced
2 Roma tomatoes, diced
1 yellow onion, diced
2 cloves of garlic, minced
1 cup low-sodium chicken broth
12 oz can tomato paste
1 tsp dried oregano
1 tsp salt
¼ tsp pepper
½ bunch fresh cilantro, stems
   and leaves
fresh steamed rice

helpful hints

Chicken breasts are much easier to slice into cubes if they are just slightly frozen.

This dish freezes extremely well. Make a double batch and reserve half to freeze for next time.

ORANGE SKILLET CHICKEN

let's do it

1 Set the rack in the center of the oven and preheat to 375 degrees.

2 Whisk together orange juice, fresh lime juice, corn syrup, honey, dry mustard, red pepper flakes and orange zest then set aside.

3 Rinse chicken breasts under cool water and pat dry with a paper towel. Trim the breasts and then season them with salt and pepper. Dredge each chicken breast in sifted flour and shake off any excess.

4 Set cast iron or oven-safe skillet over medium heat and add olive oil. When oil is shimmering, add chicken and brown each breast 3-4 minutes on each side. When the breasts are lightly browned, remove from skillet and lightly cover with aluminum foil so steam can escape. The breasts are slightly under-cooked at this point, but they'll finish in the oven. Set chicken aside to rest for just a moment.

5 Meanwhile, add onion to the skillet and cook about 3 minutes until translucent. Add juice mixture to skillet and scrape up any yummy bits left in the bottom of the pan.

6 Cook sauce about 10-15 minutes until liquid is reduced by half. If you like a thicker sauce, cook it a little longer to further reduce the liquid. Once sauce has reduced, return chicken to the skillet and turn each piece of chicken over once to ensure that they are entirely coated with glaze.

7 Transfer skillet to the oven and bake uncovered for 10-15 minutes or until the thickest part of the breast registers 165 degrees. Transfer chicken to a platter, pour the remaining glaze over it and garnish with green onion. Enjoy!

 prep time: 15 minutes

 cook time: 15 minutes

 bake time: 10-15 minutes

makes 4 servings

what you'll need

1½ cups orange juice

2 Tbsp fresh lime juice

⅓ cup light corn syrup

⅓ cup honey

¼ tsp dry mustard

¼ tsp red pepper flakes (or more to taste)

1 tsp orange zest, finely grated

½ tsp kosher salt

pinch of black pepper

4 boneless skinless chicken breasts

½ cup all-purpose flour, sifted

2 Tbsp olive oil

½ medium yellow onion, finely diced

2 Tbsp green onions, finely sliced on a diagonal

helpful hints

Watch the glaze caramelize in the oven about 7 minutes into the cooking time. As the moisture in the glaze evaporates, you'll see the sauce start to bubble and steam, producing a satin glaze on your chicken. Serve over sticky white rice for a truly Asian experience.

I'm all about using substitutions but you need to stick to this recipe and use corn syrup. It sweetens the dish and acts as a binding agent to help the sauce adhere to the flour coating on the chicken.

SAUSAGE ZUCCHINI BOATS

If you're craving yummy Italian flavor, but don't want to chow down on all the carbs, you are going to love my zucchini boats recipe. They are packed with flavor and the kids say they taste just like pizza!

let's do it

1 Set rack in the center of the oven then preheat to 375 degrees. Cut zucchini in half lengthwise then remove the seeds using a spoon—this will leave a channel along the inside of the zucchini to hold the filling. Cover zucchini with a wet paper towel then set aside.

2 Heat 2 Tbsp of olive oil in a large skillet over medium heat for about 2-3 minutes until it starts to shimmer.

3 Add the onion and then sauté for about 2-3 minutes until it becomes transparent. Then add garlic and cook for an additional 1-2 minutes.

4 Add sausage and red pepper flakes to the skillet and cook for about 8-10 minutes until the sausage is brown and fully cooked. Break sausage into small, bite-sized pieces, using a wooden spoon so that it will easily fit into your zucchini boats.

5 Drain excess fat from the pan then add tomatoes. Simmer on medium heat for about 10 minutes until most of the moisture has evaporated. You'll want a little moisture left over when you put the zucchini boats in the oven. This is because moisture will continue to evaporate from the sauce in the oven.

6 Remove the skillet from heat then transfer the mixture to a mixing bowl. Stir in the breadcrumbs and ½ cup of cheese then add salt and pepper to taste.

7 Brush the zucchini boats with olive oil then fill with equal amounts of filling. Place them onto a baking dish then sprinkle with fresh chopped basil followed by a generous amount of Parmesan cheese. Placing the Parmesan cheese on top of your fresh herbs will protect the basil from burning in the oven.

8 Bake zucchini boats uncovered for 30 minutes or until they're hot and bubbling then serve immediately and enjoy!!

 prep time: 30 minutes

 bake time: 30 minutes

 makes 12 zucchini boats

what you'll need

6 zucchini, ends trimmed

2 Tbsp olive oil

1/2 yellow onion, finely diced

1 clove garlic, chopped

1 lb sweet Italian-style chicken sausage, casings removed

1 tsp crushed red pepper flakes, if desired

14.5 oz can San Marzano tomatoes, pureed

½ cup dry breadcrumbs

1 cup grated Parmesan cheese, divided in half

salt and ground black pepper to taste

1 Tbsp chopped fresh basil (3-4 large leaves)

helpful hints

If you burn the garlic by accident, start over—there is no salvaging a dish with burned garlic!

To get your zucchini to lay flat, use a potato peeler to slice a strip off the bottom.

PORK CHOPS WITH MUSHROOM SAUCE

let's do it

1 Heat olive oil in a large skillet over medium-high heat until it starts to shimmer. Place pork chops in skillet then sear about 3 minutes per side. Allow the chops to sit undisturbed so they develop a nice golden brown crust before turning them over.

2 Transfer chops from pan to a large plate and tent loosely with a large piece of aluminum foil. Return skillet to the heat then add the shallots. You should still have about 2 Tbsp of oil in the skillet—if you need a little more, go ahead and add it now. Allow shallots to cook about 1 minute.

3 When the shallots have softened, add garlic and mushrooms. Cook 3-4 minutes until the liquid has evaporated and mushrooms begin to sizzle, then pour in the wine and continue cooking until liquid has evaporated.

4 Sprinkle flour across surface of the mushrooms then stir until flour has dissolved completely. Immediately add chicken broth, bouillon and thyme. Be sure to scrape all the yummy brown bits from the bottom of the pan and bring mixture to a boil.

5 Reduce heat to low then place the pork chops back in the plan along with any liquid that has drained onto the plate. Cover the pan and cook on low about 10 minutes, until the pork chops reach an internal temperature of 140-145 degrees.

6 Turn off heat, keeping skillet on stove, and move pork chops to a serving dish. Add cold butter to skillet and stir until it's completely incorporated—the result will be a silky, rich sauce. Remove the thyme stems from sauce and pour mixture over the pork chops. Garnish with a fresh sprig of thyme if desired and serve piping hot. Enjoy!

 prep time: 15 minutes

 cook time: 30 minutes

 makes 4 servings

what you'll need

pork chops:
2 Tbsp olive oil
4 – 1" thick boneless sirloin pork chops

mushroom sauce:
1 large or 2 small shallots, minced (approximately ¼ cup)
1 lb button or cremini mushrooms, sliced
1 clove garlic, minced
½ cup dry white wine or dry vermouth
1 Tbsp all-purpose flour
¾ cup low-sodium chicken broth
1 tsp Better than Bouillon beef flavor or 2 beef bouillon cubes
2 whole sprigs fresh thyme
3 Tbsp unsalted butter

helpful hint

To substitute the pork for chicken breasts, swap the beef bouillon for chicken bouillon then cook until the thickest part of the breast reaches 165 degrees.

BRISKET

let's do it

1 Preheat the oven to 275 degrees after placing a rack in the lower third of the oven.

2 Rinse the brisket under cool water, pat it dry with paper towels then generously season all sides of the brisket with salt and pepper.

3 Heat canola oil in a large skillet over medium-high heat then carefully add the brisket. Cook about 3-4 minutes on each side until it turns a dark shade of brown, then transfer it from the skillet to a heavy bottom Dutch oven or a roasting pan—make sure the fatty side is facing up!

4 Immediately add the onions, carrots, celery and garlic to the same skillet—the heat should still be set to medium-high. Add a bit more oil if needed. Season the veggies lightly with salt and pepper and cook 4-5 minutes, stirring occasionally.

5 Add red wine, bay leaves and thyme to the skillet and stir constantly while loosening anything that sticks to the bottom of the skillet. Boil until the wine is reduced by half, add the beef broth and bouillon to the skillet and continue to stir. Bring the mixture to a boil then remove it from the heat.

6 Pour the vegetables and broth carefully over the brisket and cover the pot with a tight-fitting lid, or seal the pan very well with aluminum foil. Place it in the oven and forget about it for about 4-5 hours.

7 When you pierce the brisket with a fork and it falls apart effortlessly, it's done! Remove it from the oven, transfer it to a cutting board and remove any excess fat from the top of the meat if you'd like. Slice the brisket against the grain into ½" thick slices and place on a serving dish.

8 Remove the vegetables from the broth to eat them as a side dish then strain the liquid through a fine mesh sieve or a colander lined with cheesecloth. Remove as much fat as possible from the top using a ladle or a defatting cup and taste the broth. If it's too salty, dilute it with a bit of water. Pour the broth over the meat and serve!

 prep time: 20 minutes

 cook time: 4-5 hours

 makes 8-10 servings

what you'll need

4-5 lb beef brisket (salt and pepper to taste)

2 Tbsp canola or vegetable oil

2 medium yellow onions, coarsely chopped

3-4 medium carrots, peeled and cut into 1" pieces

2 stalks celery, cut into 1" pieces

5 cloves garlic, peeled and crushed

1½ cup dry red wine

2 bay leaves

2 sprigs thyme

14 oz can beef broth

1 Tbsp beef bouillon

helpful hints

You'll be tempted to trim all the fat from a brisket but don't do it! Baking (braising) the brisket with the "fat cap" or fat layer facing up will allow the brisket to be essentially "basted" by the fats as they melt and move downward so there's no need to turn a brisket.

For a leaner option, cook the meat a day ahead of time and place it in the fridge, submerged in the cooking liquid. The next day, skim any excess fat and warm the meat in a 350 degree oven for 20-30 minutes.

PAN-SEARED FILET MIGNON

Pan searing steak produces a nice brown color, not to mention added flavor! Just remember to first season your steak then bring it to room temperature before cooking to soften the fibers in the meat.

let's do it

1 Season both sides of the filets with salt and let them sit at room temperature for about 1 hour or overnight in the fridge. If you season your steaks overnight, remove them from the fridge about 1 hour before cooking. Pat them dry with a paper towel before adding them to the skillet.

2 Preheat a cast iron skillet or heavy-bottom pan over high heat until very hot. Add clarified butter then press steaks into the bottom of the pan to ensure that the entire surface of the steak is in contact with the hot pan. Make sure to leave enough space between them so that they do not steam each other.

3 Allow the steaks to sear on the first side undisturbed for about 3-4 minutes. You want to allow enough time for a nice crust to form. Turn the steaks and press them into the skillet as before and allow the steaks to cook on the second side for 2 minutes.

4 Add unsalted butter, garlic and rosemary in with the steaks and allow them to cook for about 30 seconds.

5 Carefully tip the skillet (just slightly) to allow the melted butter, rosemary and garlic to move to one end and use a spoon to baste the top of the steaks with the liquid. Be sure to keep the skillet in contact with the heat as you baste. Continue basting until the steaks are cooked to the desired degree of doneness.

6 Remove the steaks from the skillet, tent them loosely with aluminum foil and allow them to rest for at least 5 minutes. Remove the foil, sprinkle the steaks with a little more salt and fresh cracked black pepper then serve.

prep time: 5 minutes

inactive prep time: 1 hour

cook time: 6-15 minutes, depending on internal temperature

makes four 4 oz servings

what you'll need

2 – 8 oz beef tenderloin filets
kosher salt or coarse sea salt (do not use table salt)
¼ cup clarified butter
2 Tbsp unsalted butter
2 garlic cloves, peeled and bruised but left whole
2 sprigs fresh rosemary
salt and freshly ground black pepper or to taste

helpful hints

Once steaks reach 5 degrees below the desired temperature, remove them from heat and let them rest 5 minutes before serving. If you cut into your steak immediately, the juices will run onto the plate, along with their flavor!

Clarified butter withstands greater temperatures than regular unsalted butter. To "clarify" your butter, gently heat the butter then pour through cheesecloth to remove the milk fat— what you're left with is clarified butter. You can also use "ghee," which is commonly used in Indian dishes.

C - Rolls

1 c milk
1 egg
4 T butter
4 T water
1/2 package (3.5 oz) inst. vanilla pudding mix
4 cup flour
1 T sugar
1/2 t salt
2 1/4 t Bread yeast

1. mix in bread machine
   Select Dough cycle
   When cycle is done remove &
   knead 3 to 5 min — Roll out
   by rectangle
2. Mix together butter brown
   sugar + cinnamon
   Spread over dough
   Roll up starting with
   wide end, Cut 1/2 in
   + 1 in slices Place in pan
   Let Rise to double
   Bake 15 & 20 Min at 350°
   make frosting + add to warm rolls

SIDE DISHES

Side dishes should definitely be able to stand alone. Once upon a time, when I was a vegetarian (another story for another time), I'd often feast or famine based on what sides were served alongside the forbidden brisket or baked chicken. Because of this experience, I like to bring variety and lots of flavor to all the sides I serve.

The sides in this chapter are perfect for family gatherings, potlucks and leftover late night snacks. (Just wait until you try the potato casserole! It definitely stands alone!)

I believe that side dishes should also be relatively easy to make. I have experienced my fair share of food fails in the kitchen, so trust me when I say the most effort should be spent on the main course. And if they do require a little bit of labor, your sides should have easy directions to follow and be well worth it!

I've done all of the heavy lifting for you in this section—no embarrassing fails on my watch! I can't wait for you to get a high-five at the dinner table.

opposite page: The house in Missouri where I grew up; mama's yeast roll recipe.

PEGGY'S POTATO CASSEROLE

My mama really shines when it comes to her potato casserole so prying the recipe out of her was a real challenge. Russets and a creamy, cheesy sauce make this dish go with just about anything.

let's do it

1 Preheat the oven to 350 degrees and spray an 8" x 8" casserole dish with cooking spray.

2 Rinse and peel each potato and place in a bowl of cold water as you slice it—this will prevent the potato from oxidizing and turning brown. Slice all of the potatoes about ⅛" to ¼" thick.

3 Next, slice the onion as thinly as possible then place it, along with the sliced potatoes in a pot of salted water. Bring to a boil over high heat then immediately reduce the heat to medium-low and simmer gently until the potatoes are cooked through but still firm.

4 While the potatoes and onions are simmering, melt the butter in a large skillet over medium heat then add the flour. Whisk until the flour has dissolved into the butter and cook for about 2 minutes, stirring constantly. Add chicken broth, whisk until smooth, then stir in milk, garlic powder, salt and pepper. Bring the mixture to a bubble, reduce heat to medium-low and simmer 5-6 minutes until the mixture has thickened.

6 Remove the skillet from heat, stir in shredded cheese and sour cream then transfer to a large bowl and set aside.

7 Drain the potatoes and onions into a colander then add them to the cheese mixture and gently stir to combine. Continue mixing gently until each potato slice is coated in the sauce. Taste the mixture and season to taste with salt and pepper. Transfer everything to the prepared casserole dish. Bake uncovered for 15 minutes, add some additional shredded cheddar cheese on top and continue to cook an additional 10-15 minutes.

8 Remove the casserole from the oven and allow the dish to rest for approximately 10 minutes before serving. Enjoy!

 prep time: 15 minutes

 cook time: 25 minutes

bake time: 25-30 minutes

 makes 9 servings

what you'll need

6 medium-sized Russet potatoes
1 yellow onion, sliced thin
3 Tbsp unsalted butter
¼ cup all-purpose flour
1½ cups chicken broth
¼ cup milk
½ tsp garlic powder
½ tsp kosher salt
¼ tsp black pepper
1 cup grated sharp cheddar cheese
    plus more for topping
½ cup sour cream
salt and pepper to taste

helpful hints

If you're a fan of potato skins you needn't peel the potatoes—it'll even save you some prep time. To minimize the bake time, par-cook the potatoes and onions in water.

Russets, also known as Idaho potatoes, are perfect for mashing or for casseroles with sauces because they are able to absorb liquids so well.

ROASTED RED SKIN POTATOES

Mix up your potato routine with my thinly sliced and roasted red skin potatoes. I used a variety of fresh herbs to make each bite equally tasty and they're a great side dish for almost any main course!

let's do it

1 Preheat the oven to 450 degrees. At the same time, place a baking sheet in the oven to heat.

2 Meanwhile, wash the potatoes and pat dry with a clean kitchen towel. Remove blemishes using a paring knife then slice the potatoes about ⅛" thick and place in a medium-sized mixing bowl.

3 Add olive oil to the potatoes and toss until each slice is completely coated. Remove the baking sheet from the oven and spread the potatoes on the baking sheet, overlapping only if necessary.

4 Sprinkle potatoes with salt and bake for 20 minutes. Then remove the potatoes from the oven and carefully flip the slices over.

5 Sprinkle with chives, garlic powder and dill then return the potatoes to the oven for an additional 10 minutes.

6 Remove the potatoes from the oven, sprinkle with fresh chopped parsley and serve immediately. Enjoy!

 prep time: 15 minutes

 bake time: 25-35 minutes

 makes 4 servings

what you'll need

1 lb red skin potatoes
1 Tbsp extra virgin olive oil
½ tsp kosher salt
1 Tbsp fresh or dried minced chives
¼ tsp garlic powder
¼ tsp fresh or dry dill
1 Tbsp fresh chopped parsley

helpful hints

I used red skin potatoes in this recipe for their comparatively low starch content. This means they'll hold their shape and have a firm, moist texture.

A mandoline slicer is the perfect tool for making uniform slices. They're widely available and there's one in just about every price range.

SPANISH RICE

My Spanish rice is a one-pot wonder that compliments any main course. I puree the tomatoes to make this dish nice and smooth, which my kiddos just love! If my kids approve, then I know it's a keeper!

let's do it

1 Puree the tomatoes along with their juices in a blender or food processor then set aside. You can also pulse the ingredients, leaving them a little chunky if you prefer more texture in your rice.

2 Add the rice to a strainer or colander then rinse well with cool water until the water runs clear. Set the strainer aside to drain completely.

3 Heat olive oil in a Dutch oven over medium-high heat until it starts to shimmer. Add onion, garlic, salt and the jalapeño if you want to add a kick of spice. Sauté the ingredients for 3-4 minutes until the onions are translucent.

4 Add rice then stir until the rice is completely coated with oil. When the grains of rice begin to swell and are opaque white in appearance, add the hot water, tomato puree and bay leaf and stir.

5 Bring everything to a boil over medium-high heat then immediately reduce the heat to low. Cover the pot with a tight-fitting lid and allow the ingredients to simmer for about 25 minutes. Resist the temptation to peek in the pot while the rice is simmering!

6 At the 25-minute mark, uncover the pot, turn off the heat and allow the rice to rest for 5 minutes. Then fluff the rice with a fork and remove the bay leaf (bay leaves make for great seasonings but they're not meant to be ingested whole). Transfer the rice to a serving dish and enjoy!

 prep time: 10 minutes

 cook time: 30 minutes

 makes 8 servings

what you'll need

14.5 oz can San Marzano tomatoes or whole peeled tomatoes
2 cups uncooked white basmati rice
¼ cup olive oil
½ medium yellow onion, finely diced
2 cloves garlic, minced
1 jalapeño, finely minced (optional)
2 cups hot water
1 bay leaf
1½ tsp kosher salt

helpful hints

After the rice has cooked for 25 minutes and it has rested, fluff the mixture by giving the contents of the pot a good stir. This will help release the steam and stop the cooking process.

Resist the temptation to sneak a peek at your rice while it cooks! Releasing the steam will change the amount of moisture in the pot.

CLOVER-SHAPED YEAST ROLLS

let's do it

1 Pour lukewarm water into the mixing bowl of a stand mixer fitted with a dough hook. Stir in yeast and ½ tsp sugar. Set aside and allow the yeast to activate in the sugar water for 10 minutes—you'll know you've activated the yeast if the mixture becomes foamy. If it doesn't become foamy, your water may be too hot or too cold or the yeast is bad and you'll need to start over!

2 Microwave milk, butter and salt in a small bowl for about 1 minute then set aside to cool. Crack the eggs into a 1 cup liquid measuring cup and add water until the measurement reaches ½ c then set aside.

3 Add 2 cups flour and ½ cup sugar to the yeast mixture and mix on low until the flour is combined, then slowly add the egg and milk mixtures. Add the remaining flour, ½ cup at a time, until the dough forms and starts to pull away from the sides of the bowl. Once this happens, increase the mixer setting to medium and mix for about 5 minutes until the dough is smooth and elastic.

4 Remove the mixing bowl from the stand mixer and add a small amount of oil to the bowl then coat the dough in oil by rolling it around in the bowl. Cover the bowl with a lint-free kitchen towel and allow the dough to rest in a warm place for 1-2 hours, or until it has doubled in size. Punch it down to deflate then roll it into a ball. Divide the dough into 72 equal-sized balls about the size of a walnut.

5 Spray 2 muffin tins with cooking spray. Place 3 dough balls into each cup of the muffin tin then cover the pans and let the dough rise for 1 more hour or until they have again doubled in size.

6 Preheat the oven to 350 degrees and bake these babies for 20-25 minutes until the tops are golden brown. Remove them from the oven, brush with melted butter and devour!

 prep time: 30 minutes

 inactive prep time: 3 hours

 bake time: 20-25 minutes

 makes 2 dozen rolls

what you'll need

1 package active dry yeast
¼ cup warm water (100-115 degrees)
½ tsp granulated sugar
1 cup warm milk
5 Tbsp unsalted butter, room temperature
1 tsp kosher salt
4½ cups all-purpose flour, divided
½ cup granulated sugar
2 eggs, room temperature
1 Tbsp vegetable oil
melted butter for brushing

helpful hints

Always have extra yeast on hand. Adding yeast to water that's too hot will kill the yeast. If this happens, the only option is to start over using new active yeast and you won't want to run to the store.

An easy way to tell when the rolls are done is to "thump" the top of one roll. If the surface is firm and sounds hollow when it's tapped, it's done!

SKILLET CORNBREAD

This cornbread is meant for eating with savory dishes such as my Texas chili on page 42 or the black bean soup on page 40. If you like it sweet like my kiddos just double the amount of sugar.

 prep time: 10 minutes

 bake time: 18-20 minutes

 makes 8 servings

let's do it

1 Place the rack in the center of the oven and preheat the oven to 400 degrees. Place your cast iron skillet on the rack to heat. Give the skillet a good while to heat—you want it sizzling hot when you add the batter!

2 Whisk the flour, cornmeal, sugar, baking soda and salt in a large mixing bowl until completely combined. In a separate bowl, beat the eggs well then whisk in the milk and buttermilk.

3 Make a well in the dry ingredients then pour the wet ingredients into the well. Stir just until the dry ingredients are moistened then gently stir in the melted butter.

4 Carefully remove the hot skillet from the oven then add the oil, giving it just a few seconds to heat up. Pour the batter into the hot pan—it will immediately begin to sizzle. Spread it evenly to the edges of the skillet and quickly return it to the oven.

5 Bake for 15-18 minutes or until it becomes a golden brown on top and the center of the cornbread is firm to the touch. Remove the skillet from the oven and set on a cooling rack. (I always put an oven mitt over the handle of the skillet to remind me that it's hot.)

6 After 10 minutes, turn pan over and place the cornbread bottom side up on a wire rack. When ready to serve, cut slices like a pizza.

what you'll need

¾ cup all-purpose flour

1¼ cups yellow cornmeal

¼ cup granulated sugar

1 tsp baking soda

1 tsp salt

2 large eggs

2/3 cup whole milk

2/3 cup buttermilk

¼ cup unsalted butter (for the batter)

2 Tbsp canola or vegetable oil
   (for the pan)

1 Tbsp unsalted butter, softened
   (for brushing the top)

helpful hints

Avoiding soap when washing your cast iron pan will keep from stripping the flavorful oils from the pan. I wash my pan with hot water and then dry it with a paper towel.

This recipe is best prepared by hand. Don't be tempted to use a mixer as it will overwork the dough, over-activate the gluten and produce a spongy texture.

LOW-CARB CAULIFLOWER MASH

I love mashed potatoes but hate the carbs, so I came up with a great low-carb alternative. A puree of cauliflower and the subtlety of leeks give me the same creamy texture I crave without all the guilt!

let's do it

1 Place the cauliflower florets and salt into a saucepan and add enough water to cover the cauliflower completely. Place the saucepan over high heat, bring the water to a full boil then immediately reduce the heat to medium-low. Simmer for approximately 6-8 minutes until it is tender and can be pierced easily with a fork.

2 Meanwhile, melt 1 Tbsp of butter in a skillet set over medium heat then add the chopped leek. Cook the leek gently for about 4-5 minutes until it's very tender—you aren't looking to brown or add any color to the leek. Make sure to stir often. Once it has softened, transfer it to a food processor and give it a few quick pulses.

3. At this point, the cauliflower should be nice and tender. Drain it and immediately return the florets to the saucepan. Return the saucepan to the heat, still set to medium-low, then begin to mash and stir the cauliflower in the pan using a wooden spoon. Continue until steam no longer rises from the pot—you want to remove the excess moisture from the cauliflower.

4 Once the excess water has been removed, transfer the cauliflower mash to the food processor and puree both the cauliflower and leek until they form a smooth puree.

5 Once the cauliflower florets and leeks are well pureed, add yogurt and the additional 2 Tbsp butter. Blend the mixture until it's silky smooth. Season with salt then serve immediately. Enjoy!

 prep time: 15 minutes

 cook time: 12 minutes

 makes 3-4 cups cauliflower mash

what you'll need

1 medium-sized head of cauliflower, cut in florets
¼ tsp salt
2 qts water (approximately)
1 leek, chopped, rinsed, green tops removed
1 Tbsp unsalted butter
2 Tbsp plain Greek yogurt or sour cream
2 Tbsp unsalted butter
salt to taste

helpful hints

Taking extra time to eliminate the excess water from the cooked cauliflower ensures that your puree will be firm rather than runny.

Leeks have a mild oniony flavor that will not overpower the delicate flavor of the cauliflower. Pureeing the leeks will give you the same creamy texture that you get from butter, but with a lot fewer calories!

SKILLET ZUCCHINI

My skillet zucchini is a yummy vegetable dish that's hearty, healthy and tastes great too. It is one of my family's favorite veggie recipes—and it can be served as a side dish or a main course!

let's do it

1 Heat olive oil in a large skillet over medium heat then cook the onions for about 5 minutes until they begin to slightly brown. Add garlic then cook for about 1 more minute.

2 Add the zucchini and diced tomatoes then pour ½ cup of chicken broth over the veggies. Stir in sugar and herbs then reduce the heat to low.

3 Cook, stirring often, for about 2-2 ½ hours, adding more chicken broth as needed to increase the moisture. As the dish nears the final stages of cooking, season to taste with salt and pepper.

4 Dish it up while it's hot and enjoy!

 prep time: 10 minutes

 cook time: 2-2½ hours

 makes 8 servings

what you'll need

3 Tbsp extra virgin olive oil
2 yellow onions, finely diced
3-5 zucchini, sliced about ¼" thick
3 cloves garlic, minced
2 - 16 oz cans diced tomatoes
14.5 oz can chicken broth
1 tsp granulated sugar
1 tsp dried basil
1 tsp dried oregano leaves
1 tsp dried thyme
salt and pepper to taste

helpful hints

Season this dish toward the end of the cooking process. This will prevent it from becoming too salty and from breaking down the vegetables.

Zucchini can vary widely in size. For optimum flavor, use zucchini that are a slightly smaller than a cucumber.

ROASTED BRUSSELS SPROUTS WITH SLICED ALMONDS

If you like Brussels sprouts, you are going to love this recipe. Seasoned, roasted and caramelized to perfection, this side dish is easy to prep, cook and serve! My kiddos call Brussels sprouts tiny cabbages.

let's do it

1 Set the baking rack in the center of the oven then preheat the oven to 375 degrees.

2 Place the trimmed Brussels sprouts in a medium-sized bowl then drizzle with olive oil. Toss sprouts in oil until they are completely coated then sprinkle with kosher salt.

3 Transfer the Brussels sprouts to baking sheet then sprinkle almonds and minced garlic over the top.

4 Bake Brussels sprouts uncovered for 25-30 minutes or until the leaves are dark brown, caramelized and easily pierced with a sharp knife.

5 Remove sprouts from the oven then sprinkle with Parmesan cheese. Serve and chow down!

 prep time: 5 minutes

 bake time: 25-30 minutes

 makes 2-4 servings

what you'll need
20-24 Brussels sprouts, trimmed
1 ½ Tbsp light olive oil
½ tsp kosher salt
¼ cup sliced natural almonds
1 clove of garlic, minced
Parmesan cheese, grated (optional)

helpful hints
Brussels sprouts are readily available all year round, but their prime season is August through February.

Trim Brussels sprouts by washing them in a colander then remove any bruised or yellowed leaves. Slice off the rough part of the stem and voila—you're ready for action!

ROASTED CAULIFLOWER BITES

I love recipes that serve double-duty as a side or starter. My seasoned cauliflower florets are lightly coated with Parmesan and breadcrumbs. I often serve this tasty dish as an after school snack for the kids.

let's do it

1 Preheat the oven to 450 degrees after moving a rack to the bottom third of the oven. Line a baking sheet with aluminum foil and spray lightly with olive oil cooking spray.

2 Stir the melted butter, garlic powder, salt and pepper in a large mixing bowl then add the cauliflower florets. Toss until each floret is completely coated with butter and spices then set aside.

3 Mix the Parmesan cheese and breadcrumbs together in a separate bowl. Add 5 or 6 of the buttered florets into the Parmesan/breadcrumb mixture and coat each one completely—try to obtain as much breading as possible on the cauliflower.

4 Transfer the breaded florets to the prepared baking sheet and repeat until all of the florets have been breaded. Space them on the baking sheet evenly but as far apart as possible so they don't steam.

5 Spray the cauliflower lightly with cooking spray then bake 18-22 minutes, turning once halfway through.

6 Remove these yummy bites from the oven when they're fork tender and golden brown. Cool slightly before serving. Enjoy!

 prep time: 15 minutes

 bake time: 18-22 minutes

makes 8 servings

what you'll need

olive oil cooking spray

1 large head cauliflower,
    cut into florets

5 Tbsp unsalted butter, melted

¾ tsp garlic powder

½ tsp salt

¼ tsp black pepper

⅔ cup Parmesan cheese, finely grated

⅓ cup fine breadcrumbs or panko

helpful hints

Be sure to fill all of the little nooks and crannies of the cauliflower with the butter and the breadcrumb/Parmesan mixture for the best flavor!

Delete the breadcrumbs for a lower-carb dish. It'll still taste great!

QUICK SAUTÉED GREEN BEANS WITH LEMON & GARLIC

Fresh green beans make all the difference when it comes to a sautéed side. I like mine crispy, so I boil them for 5 minutes then "shock" them in an ice bath to prevent overcooking and to keep their bright color.

let's do it

1 Bring 6 cups of water to a boil in a large pot over high heat. While the water is heating, fill a large mixing bowl half full of ice water and set it aside.

2 When the water has reached a boil, gently add the green beans then reduce heat to medium-low and simmer for 5 minutes.

3 When the beans are as tender as you would like them, drain the water and transfer the beans immediately into the bowl of ice water.

4 Once the beans are completely cool, remove the ice, drain the water once again and set the beans aside.

5 Next, melt the butter in a large skillet over medium heat, then add garlic and cook until the edges just begin to brown (about 2 minutes).

6 Stir in lemon juice, lemon zest, salt and red pepper flakes, heating until the liquid begins to bubble. Immediately add green beans and toss them in the lemon butter mixture to coat. Cook for about 2 minutes, just long enough to heat the beans all the way through.

7 Transfer beans from the skillet to a serving bowl, sprinkle with Parmesan cheese and fresh black pepper then serve them right away! Enjoy!

 prep time: 10 minutes

 cook time: 10-12 minutes

makes 5-6 servings

what you'll need

1 lb fresh green beans, ends trimmed
2 Tbsp unsalted butter
1 clove garlic, sliced thinly
1 Tbsp lemon juice (about ½ lemon)
zest from ½ lemon, finely grated
½ tsp salt
¼ tsp red pepper flakes (optional)
2 Tbsp Parmesan, shredded or grated
freshly ground black pepper

helpful hints

Slicing garlic thinly but in larger pieces will actually give your finished dish a more subtle garlic flavor. Plus, it's much easier to remove if someone in your family is averse to garlic.

A microplane is so easy to hold and simply the best tool for grating citrus zest and hard cheeses such as Parmesan.

EASY CREAMED SPINACH

This side is so darn delicious, super easy and only takes 15 minutes to make! It can also double as a dip. I just add Parmesan and a can of drained artichoke hearts while the spinach is hot and serve it warm with crusty bread or bagel chips. Yum!

let's do it

1 Add spinach and water to a skillet over medium heat. Cook, tossing occasionally, for about 3–4 minutes until the spinach is wilted and bright green. Remove from the heat then transfer the spinach to a colander.

2 Press the spinach against the sides of the colander using the back of a spoon, to remove as much liquid as possible. This is an important step—if you're not thorough with this process, the final product will be watery. When you've squeezed all of the liquid from the spinach, move it from the colander to the cutting board, chop the spinach coarsely then set aside.

3 Return the skillet to medium-low heat to melt the butter. When it has melted, add onion or shallot and cook 3-4 minutes until tender and translucent.

4 Add flour then stir for about 1 minute until it has dissolved into the butter. Then add milk, stirring again until the flour is completely dissolved and smooth.

5 Add bay leaf, salt, pepper and the optional nutmeg.

6 Heat until the mixture begins to bubble and thicken, then reduce the heat to low. Let it simmer 2-3 minutes, stirring constantly. It's important to be patient as the sauce cooks on a low heat setting—you don't want to scorch the cream sauce!

7 Add spinach to the cream sauce, stirring to incorporate. Cook until the spinach is heated through and the dish reaches the desired consistency. Remove the bay leaf, transfer to a serving dish and enjoy!

 prep time: 5 minutes

 cook time: 15 minutes

 makes 4 servings

what you'll need

16 oz fresh baby spinach
¼ c water
2 Tbsp unsalted butter
2 Tbsp finely minced onion or shallot
2 Tbsp all-purpose flour
1 cup whole milk
1 small bay leaf
½ tsp salt
dash pepper
dash nutmeg (optional)

helpful hints

A pound of baby spinach might seem like a lot, but once it's cooked down and the liquid has been pressed out, you'll find that you're left with slightly less than 1 cup of cooked spinach.

If your finished product is too thick, just add a little milk until you get the desired consistency.

GLAZED SWEET CARROTS

Everyone loves carrots, especially when they are cooked in a sweet glaze of butter, brown sugar and cinnamon. The best thing about this dish is that there's only one pan to clean!

let's do it

1 Place carrots into a medium-sized skillet then add just enough water to completely cover the carrots. Move the skillet to the stove and bring to a boil over medium-high heat. Once the water has begun to boil, reduce the heat to medium-low and simmer for about 6-8 minutes until the carrots are very tender but not mushy.

2 Remove the skillet from the heat and drain off any remaining water, leaving the carrots in the pan.

3 Return the skillet to the heat, which should be set to medium-low. Add butter, brown sugar and salt to the carrots. Gently stir to coat the carrots with the sugar mixture and cook until the sugar and butter have formed a syrupy consistency that glazes the carrots—it'll only take a few minutes.

4 Remove from heat once the glaze has formed. Sprinkle lightly with a pinch of salt and cinnamon then stir once again. Transfer to a serving dish and enjoy!

 prep time: 5 minutes

 cook time: 15 minutes

 makes 4-6 servings

what you'll need

1 lb carrots, peeled and cut on the
    diagonal into equal pieces
1 Tbsp unsalted butter
2 Tbsp brown sugar
½ tsp kosher salt
1 pinch ground cinnamon

helpful hints

The amount of time it takes to cook your carrots varies according to how thick they've been cut. To test, pierce the thickest part of a carrot using the tip of a paring knife. When it pierces easily, it's done.

Cutting carrots into uniform-sized pieces allows for more even cooking. Make it easy on yourself—buy a bag of baby carrots for virtually no prep!

FRESH CORN CASSEROLE

Call it pudding, soufflé or casserole—I call it awesome! This is one comfort food that's sweet, light and fluffy like a dessert, super easy to make and pretty much fail-proof.

let's do it

1 Preheat your oven to 350 degrees and grease an 8" square casserole dish or 9" deep dish pie pan with a little bit of butter.

2 Whisk the sugar, flour, baking powder and salt together in a small bowl just until uniformly combined—there shouldn't be any visible clumps of flour. Set aside.

3 In a large mixing bowl, whisk the eggs, whipping cream and melted butter together until fully incorporated. Add the corn kernels then stir until combined.

4 Add the dry ingredients to the corn mixture, whisking until completely smooth. Then transfer the corn custard into your baking dish.

5. Bake for 45-50 minutes. You'll know it's done when the top of the corn soufflé turns a beautiful golden brown. The center will wobble slightly when jiggled and the top will be just firm to the touch.

6 Remove the casserole from the oven and allow it to rest 5 minutes before indulging!

 prep time: 15 minutes

 bake time: 45-50 minutes

 makes 9 servings

what you'll need

2 Tbsp granulated sugar

1 ½ Tbsp flour

1 tsp baking powder

¾ tsp salt

3 large eggs

1 cup whipping cream

¼ cup unsalted butter, melted

4 cups fresh corn kernels, removed from cob (about 8 ears) or 4 cups frozen kernels, defrosted

helpful hints

To remove the kernels from the cobs, cut off one end of each cob and stand it upright on a cutting board. Hold it by the top and slice off the kernels in a downward motion using a chef's knife.

Like more corn and less "casserole"? Add an extra cup of corn—it won't hurt the baking time and you won't need to adjust any of the other ingredients.

Italian Cream Cake

2 cups sugar
1 stick oleo, ½ cup Crisco (cream well beg
5 egg yolks (add one at a time)
2 cups flour, 1 tsp soda, 1 cup buttermilk
1 can cocoanut (2 cups)
1 tsp vanilla
        Beat all together & fold in 5 egg
whites beaten stiff. Bake in 4 8" layers or
4 9" layers 30 min at 350°
                                    over

Icing

1 8 oz pkg cream cheese   1 tsp vanilla
1 stick oleo   ½ cup chopped nuts
1 box powdered sugar

    Soften cheese and oleo and beat together
in mixer until smooth. Add powdered
sugar, vanilla and mix well. Stir in
nuts. Spread on cool cake

SWEET ENDINGS

I have to admit that this entire chapter could have been filled with cookie dough recipes. I cannot pass up the opportunity to eat cookie dough. In fact, I often have no interest in the finished product once it becomes a cookie and have been known to hoard and hide containers of the prized sweet to keep all to myself. But since I can't write an entire chapter about dough, I figured the next best thing would be to share all the cakes, pies and cookies that I loved so much when I was growing up.

My favorite cooked dessert in the whole world is coconut cream pie. My mom would make a pie for my birthday every year and I would get the treat of having the whole pie to myself. I didn't have to share even one single slice. And although I would love nothing more than to devour a whole pie alone like I did as a child, I need to have a little more restraint now. So, I prepare my mama's recipe using individual-sized ramekins so that I get the pleasure of having it all to myself, but the portion is just a tad bit smaller. The kids love the ramekins too. It just seems so much more fun to eat a pie that is all your own. Try it out and see what you think!

opposite page: Two-year-old Cheryl and bouffant Peggy. Wait until you try this Italian cream cake recipe. Look at the vanilla splatters on this well-loved recipe card!

INDIVIDUAL COCONUT CREAM PIES

let's do it

1 Add enough broken vanilla wafers to cover the bottoms of 6 individual ramekins and set aside.

2 To make the custard, add sugar, cornstarch and salt. Use a whisk to combine the ingredients and remove the lumps. Then add milk and egg yolks and whisk to blend the ingredients completely.

3 Place the saucepan over medium heat and stir constantly until the mixture comes to a boil. Continue stirring and allow to boil for 1 minute then remove the pan from heat—the custard should have started to form and thickened quite a bit. Then stir in the coconut, vanilla extract and butter.

4 Next, distribute the mixture evenly among the ramekins. Cover the ramekins with plastic wrap to prevent a skin from forming and cool the pies completely in the fridge.

5 To make the meringue, first check to make sure there's not a speck of yolk left in your egg whites. Then whip the egg whites and cream of tartar in a perfectly clean, grease-free bowl on high speed, until foam begins to form.

6 Slowly begin adding sugar while beating on high speed for several minutes, until stiff peaks form and all of the sugar is incorporated—the meringue should be fluffy and glossy.

7 Once you've made the meringue, remove the plastic wrap from the ramekins and pipe or spoon the meringue on top of the filling. Sprinkle the top of the meringue with toasted coconut and serve. Everyone will think you've been slaving away in the kitchen all day!

 prep time: 20 minutes

 cook time: 5 minutes

 makes 6 individual-sized pies

what you'll need

12-14 vanilla wafer cookies, broken into pieces
½ cup granulated sugar
3 Tbsp cornstarch
½ tsp salt
3 cups whole milk
3 eggs, separated (you'll use both the yolks and whites)
1 cup shredded, sweetened coconut
1 tsp pure vanilla extract
1 Tbsp unsalted butter, room temperature
⅛ tsp cream of tartar
⅓ cup granulated sugar
½ cup shredded coconut, toasted

helpful hints

If a few lumps bother you when making the custard, press the filling through a fine mesh strainer before stirring in the coconut, vanilla extract and butter.

For perfectly toasted coconut, scatter the shavings on a baking sheet and bake for 8 minutes at 350 degrees, stirring every 2 minutes to ensure that it toasts evenly. A toaster oven works, too!

PECAN TART

My pecan tart wouldn't taste so darn good without my mama's legendary pie crust recipe. Combine the two and you have a dessert that will be devoured in a fraction of the time it took to make!

let's do it

1 To make the crust, sift the flour, sugar and salt into a medium-sized mixing bowl then add water and oil, mixing until the ingredients are blended completely. Roll the mixture into a ball then allow it to rest for 5-10 minutes at room temperature.

2 Next, roll the dough out between 2 sheets of wax paper until you have a diameter roughly 1" wider than the tart pan. Transport the dough to the pan, remove the top layer of wax paper and then invert the dough into the tart pan.

3 Carefully peel off the remaining piece of wax paper, then ease the dough into the corners of the pan. Trim excess dough from the edges using a butter knife and place the tart pan in the refrigerator until the filling is prepared.

4 Place a rack in the center of your oven and preheat to 325 degrees. To prepare the pecan filling, whisk the eggs in a medium-sized mixing bowl until they're well beaten but not foamy.

5 Add the sugar, light and dark corn syrup and melted butter, stirring until thoroughly combined. Add salt and vanilla then mix in the pecans.

6 Grab the tart pan from the refrigerator then place it on a baking sheet. Pour the pecan filling into the pan then bake for 50-60 minutes, until the filling is set in the center and the crust is light golden brown.

7 Remove from the oven then cool to room temperature. Slice, serve and enjoy!

 prep time: 30 minutes

 bake time: 50-60 minutes

 makes one 9" pecan tart

what you'll need

mama's pie crust:
2 cups all-purpose flour
pinch sugar
½ tsp salt
½ cup vegetable or canola oil
¼ cup cold water

pecan filling:
3 large eggs, room temperature
⅔ cup granulated sugar
½ cup light corn syrup
½ cup dark corn syrup
⅓ cup unsalted butter, melted
¼ tsp vanilla extract
dash of salt
2 cups pecans, coarsely chopped
    or whole

helpful hints

Rolling out your dough between two pieces of wax paper will prevent it from being over-handled, keep it from tearing and make it easier to transfer to your pan.

Working with corn syrup can be messy. Avoid kitchen chaos by spritzing your measuring cup with cooking spray—the corn syrup will slip right out!

CLASSIC CUSTARD PIE

Custard pie is one of my all time favorite desserts, especially when it's made with a homemade crust and a premium vanilla extract, plus Mama's pie crust works well for any recipe that needs a crust.

let's do it

1 To make the pie crust, you'll need to preheat the oven to 375 degrees. Add all the dry ingredients to a medium-sized mixing bowl then stir to combine.

2 Add the oil and water then mix together until a dough forms. Once it has formed, shape it into a ball, wrap it in plastic then allow it to rest at least 5-10 minutes in the fridge.

3 Remove the chilled dough from the fridge and roll it out between 2 sheets of wax paper to keep it from sticking to your rolling pin. Once the dough's rolled, simply place it in the pie pan, crimp or flute the edges and refrigerate until ready to use.

4 Meanwhile, get started on your custard by beating eggs with vanilla, sugar and salt in a large mixing bowl. Stir in the milk then pour the mixture through a strainer into the unbaked pie crust. Don't forget to sprinkle it with a little nutmeg, cinnamon or mace.

5 Bake the pie for 35-40 minutes. You'll want to start checking for doneness at 30 minutes because you don't want the filling to bubble. You'll know it's done when the center of the pie is still a bit wobbly but no longer liquid.

6 Chill at least 4 hours or overnight before serving.

 prep time: 15 minutes

 bake time: 35-40 minutes

 makes one 9" deep-dish pie

what you'll need

mama's pie crust:
2 cups all-purpose flour
pinch of sugar
½ tsp salt
½ cup vegetable oil
¼ cup cold water

custard:
5 large eggs
1 Tbsp pure vanilla extract
1 cup granulated sugar
¼ tsp salt
3 cups whole milk
sprinkle of nutmeg, cinnamon or mace

helpful hints

As with any custard, it's a good idea to pour it through a strainer in case there's an occasional eggshell. There are also parts of the egg that won't break down no matter how hard you beat them—this step will remove them both.

Use the absolute finest vanilla you can afford. Real vanilla has greater depth and complexity. There are three main types of vanilla: Madagascar Bourbon (named after the Bourbon islands, not the liquor), Tahitian (fruity) and Mexican (spicy).

PUDDIN' 'N' PIE

This sweet and salty dessert has been passed down from my mama to me and has survived the test of time!

let's do it

1 Place rack in the center of the oven then preheat to 350 degrees. Spray a 9" x 13" cake pan with cooking spray then set aside.

2 To make the crust, pulse pecans in a food processor until they are finely chopped. Add flour, 2 Tbsp sugar and salt then pulse a few more times until the ingredients are just combined. Pour in 1 stick of melted butter and pulse until a coarse paste has formed. Press crust evenly into the bottom of cake pan then place it in oven for 10-12 minutes until crust is golden brown. Remove pan from oven and cool completely.

3 Meanwhile, beat cream cheese until smooth then add 1 cup powdered sugar and mix until combined. Allow mixture to sit at room temperature while you prepare the pudding and whipped cream.

4 For the pudding, whisk ¾ cup granulated sugar, cornstarch and salt in a small saucepan, away from heat, until no lumps remain. Whisk in egg yolks followed immediately by whole milk and evaporated milk. Transfer saucepan to stove and cook over medium heat, stirring constantly until liquid comes to a bubble. Once you see the first bubble burst on the surface of the pudding, cook 1 minute longer, stirring constantly.

5 Remove pudding from heat then immediately whisk in 3 Tbsp butter and 1 Tbsp vanilla. Pour liquid into a bowl then place a sheet of plastic wrap directly onto the surface—this will prevent a film from forming on the surface. Refrigerate at least 30 minutes.

6 To make the whipped cream, add heavy whipping cream, ¼ cup powdered sugar and 1 tsp vanilla to a mixing bowl then whip on high speed until stiff peaks form. Cover and refrigerate until you're ready to assemble your puddin' 'n' pie.

7 Once pudding and crust are cool, spread cream cheese over crust, followed by the pudding, then the whipped cream—all in even layers. Allow the pie to chill in the fridge 2-3 hours, then cut and serve!

 prep time: 45 minutes

 cook time: 25 minutes

 inactive prep time: 2-3 hours

 makes 12 servings

what you'll need

crust:
2 cups chopped pecans
1 cup all-purpose flour
2 Tbsp granulated sugar
½ tsp salt
½ cup (1 stick) unsalted butter, melted

cream cheese layer:
8 oz package cream cheese
1 cup powdered sugar

pudding layer:
¾ cup granulated sugar
6 Tbsp cornstarch
¼ tsp salt
7 egg yolks
3 cups whole milk (do NOT use anything less than whole milk)
¾ cup evaporated milk
1 Tbsp pure vanilla extract or vanilla bean paste
3 Tbsp unsalted butter

whipped cream:
2 cups (1 pint) heavy whipping cream
¼ cup powdered sugar
1 tsp pure vanilla extract

ITALIAN CREAM CAKE

let's do it

1 Place the rack in the center of the oven then preheat to 350 degrees. Line the bottom of 3 – 8" or 9" round cake pans with parchment paper then spray each pan with cooking spray.

2 In a large mixing bowl, cream 2 cups of sugar, 1 stick of butter and ½ cup margarine or vegetable shortening until ingredients are light and fluffy. Beat in egg yolks, 1 at a time, until incorporated.

3 Next, mix in buttermilk, coconut and 1 tsp vanilla until combined. Sift flour and baking soda into batter then fold the mixture until well combined.

4 Divide batter equally into three pans. A kitchen scale is the easiest way to divide the batter among the pans, but if you don't have one, just eyeball it! You'll want to make sure the measurements are somewhat accurate—otherwise the cook times for each pan will vary.

5 Bake 25-30 minutes, until toothpick comes out clean and the sides of cake begin to pull away from pan. Remove cakes from oven then place on a cooling rack, allowing them to cool in the pan for 10 minutes. After 10 minutes, remove cakes from pans and continue to cool.

6 To make the icing, beat cream cheese and 1 stick of butter in a mixing bowl until ingredients are completely smooth. Sift in powdered sugar and beat until mixture is light and fluffy—then stir in vanilla and pecans.

7 When icing is complete and cake layers have cooled, remove parchment paper from bottom of each cake. Stack the cakes—spreading about ½ cup of icing between each layer—then coat exterior completely with remaining icing. Allow cake to rest about 1 hour then slice, serve and enjoy!

 prep time: 40 minutes

 bake time: 25-30 minutes

 makes one 8" layer cake

what you'll need

cake:
2 cups granulated sugar

½ cup (1 stick) unsalted butter, softened

½ cup margarine or vegetable shortening

5 egg yolks

1 cup buttermilk

2 cups shredded, sweetened coconut

1 tsp pure vanilla extract

2 cups all-purpose flour

1 tsp baking soda

icing:
8 oz cream cheese, softened

½ cup (1 stick) unsalted butter, softened

1 lb box powdered sugar

1 tsp pure vanilla extract

½ cup chopped pecans

helpful hint

Reserve the egg whites and freeze them for up to 6 months by placing them in an ice cube tray. Once they are frozen, transfer them to a freezer-safe resealable bag. Make sure to put a date on the bag!

CRUNCHY MUNCHIES

Okay, I'll admit it—I like to eat the cookie dough more than the cookies themselves! Most cookie dough is better if it rests overnight in the fridge—it actually enhances the flavor but whenever I open the door, I find it too darn hard to resist!

let's do it

1 Preheat the oven to 350 degrees and line a baking sheet with parchment paper.

2 Lightly whisk together the flour, salt, baking soda and cinnamon in a medium-sized bowl then set aside.

3 Blend the butter, granulated sugar and brown sugar on low speed until light and fluffy, using a stand mixer or hand mixer. Add the eggs, one at a time, beating after each addition. Mix in the vanilla and scrape the sides of the bowl to ensure that everything is incorporated.

4 Add the flour mixture and blend on low, until the flour is completely combined. Add the oats and almonds, mix well then add the cornflakes to the bowl—fold them in by hand so they don't get crushed!

5 Drop golf ball-sized amounts of cookie dough onto the parchment-lined baking sheet. Flatten the cookie dough just a bit with your fingers (and dip them in water as needed to keep them from sticking to the baking sheet!).

6 Bake 10-12 minutes until the cookies are brown around the edges and firm in the center (under-bake them a few minutes if chewier cookies are preferred). Cool the cookies on the baking sheet for 5 minutes then transfer them to a rack to cool completely before scarfing them down. Yum!

 prep time: 20 minutes

 bake time: 10-12 minutes

 makes 2 dozen cookies

what you'll need

1½ cups all-purpose flour

1 tsp salt

1 tsp baking soda

1 tsp ground cinnamon

1 cup (2 sticks) unsalted butter, at room temperature

⅔ cup granulated sugar

⅔ cup brown sugar, firmly packed

2 eggs, room temperature

1 tsp pure vanilla extract

2 cups old-fashioned oats (not quick or instant)

1 cup sliced raw almonds

2 cups uncrushed cornflakes

helpful hints

Oven temperatures vary so adjust your baking sheets by rotating halfway or switching racks to ensure cookies brown evenly.

If your butter's straight from the fridge, place it in the microwave for 15-20 seconds to soften but not melt—you don't want oily cookies!

MAMA'S THIN & CRISPY SUGAR COOKIES

My mama's cookies are light, crispy and so delicate they practically melt in your mouth! They're easy to make and are great served alongside my fruit salad on page 135.

let's do it

1 Preheat the oven to 325 degrees and line a cookie sheet with parchment paper.

2 Sift the flour, baking powder and salt into a large mixing bowl then set aside.

3 Cream the sugar, powdered sugar, butter and oil in a separate bowl until light and fluffy. Add the vanilla and eggs one at a time, beating well after each addition.

4 Combine the wet and dry ingredients and mix until combined.

5 Next, form the cookie dough into golf ball-sized balls and roll in granulated sugar. Place the balls about 3"-4" apart on a cookie sheet. You may only be able to fit 8 or 9 cookies on a cookie sheet at a time but that's okay—once these cookies are flattened out, they take up quite a bit of space!

6 Flatten the balls on the cookie sheet, using the bottom of a glass but first dip the bottom into a small plate of sugar. This will keep the glass from sticking to the cookies. Flatten the cookie to approximately ⅛" thick—you want these cookies to be really thin so they'll be crispy!

7 Bake 10-12 minutes until lightly browned on the bottom and edges but not on top. Cool on a wire rack and enjoy!

 prep time: 15 minutes

 bake time: 10-12 minutes

 makes 3 dozen cookies

what you'll need

5¼ cups all-purpose flour

1 tsp baking powder

1 tsp salt

1 cup granulated sugar

1 cup powdered sugar

1 cup (2 sticks) unsalted butter, softened

1 cup vegetable oil

1 tsp pure vanilla extract

2 large eggs, room temperature

¼ cup granulated sugar (for coating)

helpful hints

For a silkier cookie, sift your powdered sugar after you measure it—it's notorious for clumping together!

If your cookie is soft and chewy, bake the next batch a little longer but be careful to brown only the sides and edges, not the top.

CHOCOLATE ZUCCHINI CAKE

My fridge usually has an overabundance of zucchini in the summertime so I'm always looking for new ways to use it. Indulging myself with this super moist zucchini cake with cocoa and a chocolate glaze is pure satisfaction!

let's do it

1 Place a rack in the bottom third of the oven and preheat to 350 degrees. Butter and flour a Bundt pan then set aside.

2 Sift the flour, baking powder, baking soda, salt and cocoa powder into a large bowl to remove any lumps, then set aside.

3 In a separate mixing bowl, add eggs and beat on high speed for about 2-3 minutes with a hand mixer while gradually adding the sugar. The mixture will be pale yellow in color and have a thick, creamy consistency.

4 Next, add the oil, applesauce and melted butter and beat thoroughly.

5 Add the flour mixture to the egg mixture and fold gently by hand until combined.

6 Stir in shredded zucchini then pour the batter evenly into prepared Bundt pan. (If you are like me and love any uncooked batter or dough you'll want to lick the spatula clean!)

7 Bake for 1 hour before testing for doneness. The cake may take up to 75 minutes to bake but you'll know it's done when a toothpick comes out with moist crumbs attached.

8 Remove the cake from the oven and allow it to cool for approximately 20 minutes before removing it from the pan. Cool completely.

9 If you want to add a glaze, simply microwave store-bought chocolate frosting until it reaches a thick but pourable consistency. Enjoy!

 prep time: 20 minutes

 bake time: 60-75 minutes

 makes 1 Bundt cake

what you'll need

3 cups all-purpose flour
1½ tsp baking powder
1 tsp baking soda
1 tsp salt
½ cup cocoa powder
4 large eggs, room temperature
3 cup granulated sugar
1 cup vegetable or canola oil
½ cup applesauce
3 Tbsp unsalted butter, melted
3 cups shredded zucchini, packed
your favorite store-bought chocolate frosting for glaze (optional)

helpful hints

Three cups of packed, shredded zucchini is the equivalent of two cucumber-sized zucchini.

When testing a cake, test the thickest part of the cake: the center. You want the cake tester or toothpick to have crumbs on it. If the toothpick comes out clean, it means the cake is a little over-baked—but this cake is so moist, no one will notice!

SOCK IT TO ME CAKE

I like to keep this recipe on hand for times when I'm too rushed to make cake from scratch. This recipe is an old classic from my grandma that I've adjusted to my family's liking. It's super moist and easy to make and keeps fresh for 2-3 days. In fact, I feel it tastes better after the second day!

let's do it

1 Preheat the oven to 325 degrees and generously grease a Bundt pan with cooking spray.

2 Add the cake mix to a large mixing bowl then stir in oil and ¼ cup granulated sugar. Stir in eggs, 1 at a time, and then add the sour cream and vanilla. Beat using a hand mixer or a stand mixer on high speed for about 2 minutes.

3 In a separate bowl, combine pecans with the brown sugar and cinnamon then set aside.

4 Pour half of the batter into the prepared Bundt pan. Sprinkle the pecan sugar mixture over the entire surface then pour in the remaining batter.

5 Bake for 1 hour or until a cake tester comes out clean.

6 Remove cake from the oven, cover Bundt pan with a lint-free towel and allow it to cool for at least 20 minutes. Then invert the cake onto a plate, slice, serve and enjoy!

 prep time: 10 minutes

 bake time: 1 hour

 makes 1 Bundt cake

what you'll need

1 golden butter cake mix
¾ cup vegetable oil
¼ cup granulated sugar
4 large eggs, room temperature
1 cup sour cream
1 Tbsp pure vanilla extract
1 cup chopped pecans
3 Tbsp brown sugar
1½ Tbsp ground cinnamon

helpful hints

Starting this recipe with a cake mix makes it quick and super easy. Just be sure to use a butter recipe cake mix for that extra rich flavor!

Make sure to thoroughly grease your Bundt pan—releasing the cake from the pan will be easier. It also helps to cool the cake in the pan for at least 20 minutes before inverting it.

CHEWY CRUNCHY BROWNIES

It's hard to believe that some people aren't crazy about chocolate but I'm definitely not one of them! I teamed mellow Dutch-process chocolate with pecans for the ultimate chewy, crunchy brownie.

 prep time: 15 minutes

 bake time: 35-40 minutes

 makes 2 dozen brownies

let's do it

1 Place a rack in the center of the oven and preheat to 350 degrees. Spray a 9" x 13" glass baking dish with cooking spray then set aside.

2 Whisk the Dutch-process cocoa powder, warm melted butter, hot water and oil together in a medium-sized mixing bowl until completely blended. Scrape the sides of your bowl with a rubber spatula in order to incorporate all of the ingredients.

3 Add the eggs, yogurt and vanilla to the cocoa mixture (if you're out of yogurt, you can substitute sour cream). Continue to whisk until everything is smooth and creamy. Whisk in the granulated sugar and mix until it's blended completely.

4 Sift the flour and salt over the top of the wet ingredients and mix just until combined, but don't overwork the batter! Again, scrape the sides of the bowl and make certain all of the ingredients have incorporated.

5 Fold in the pecan pieces then transfer the batter to the prepared baking dish.

6 Bake 35-40 minutes until a toothpick comes out with just a few moist crumbs attached and the top is firm to the touch. Allow the brownies to cool for an hour before dusting them with powdered sugar. Cut into large squares and serve.

what you'll need

¾ cup Dutch-process cocoa (not natural cocoa)

5 Tbsp unsalted butter, melted and still warm

½ cup plus 2 Tbsp boiling water

½ cup plus 2 Tbsp vegetable oil

2 large eggs, room temperature

3 Tbsp Greek yogurt

2 tsp pure vanilla extract

2½ cups granulated sugar

1¾ cups all-purpose flour

¼ tsp kosher salt

½ cup chopped pecans

powdered sugar for dusting (optional)

helpful hints

Dutch-process cocoa does not react with baking soda due to the neutralization of its natural acidity so it is NOT interchangeable with natural cocoa.

When baking, all of your ingredients should be at room temperature. This not only makes the batter come together much easier, but the brownies will bake much more evenly if the batter isn't cold.

GRAHAM CRACKER BITES

Sometimes it isn't just my kids who crave something sweet—it's me too! These candies are super easy to make, especially if you use a food processor. You'll have the perfect blend of savory and sweet.

let's do it

1 Grind approximately 2 packages of graham crackers in a food processor to form fine crumbs—you should make enough crumbs to equal 2½ cups. Transfer the cracker crumbs into a medium-sized mixing bowl.

2 Add sweetened condensed milk, vanilla extract and salt to the graham cracker crumbs. Mix until completely combined.

3 Scoop out the mixture using a tablespoon or small cookie scoop and roll into balls—I make them about the size of ping-pong balls but you can make them any size you'd like!

4 Place the balls on a parchment-lined baking sheet, cover them with plastic wrap and refrigerate until they are firm.

5 Melt the chocolate chips or chocolate melts in the microwave until smooth. Remove the balls from the fridge and drop them, one at a time, into the melted chocolate—use a fork to completely coat each candy.

6 Carefully place the coated bites on parchment paper then immediately sprinkle with kosher or sea salt. Allow the candies to sit at room temperature until the chocolate sets—it won't take long.

7 Once the chocolate has set, you're ready to dig in!

 prep time: 30 minutes

 inactive prep time: 30 minutes

 makes 36 candies

what you'll need

2 packages graham crackers, crushed finely (approximately 2½ cups)
14 oz can sweetened condensed milk
½ tsp pure vanilla extract
¼ tsp fine sea salt
1 bag dark chocolate chips or chocolate melts (for dipping)
coarse sea salt or kosher salt for sprinkling

helpful hints

You can replace the graham crackers with your favorite cookie...the kids will love Oreos too.

Unless you are adept at tempering chocolate, using chocolate chips or chocolate melts is the way to go— they're formulated to re-harden after being melted.

SWEET & SALTY CRUNCH

Forget your old party mix made with cereal—I've got a recipe that's the perfect blend of sweet and salty for your next gathering. It takes minutes to make and is a favorite in our house! I detect a sweet and salty theme here!

let's do it

1 Preheat the oven to 325 degrees after moving 2 oven racks to the middle positions. Line 2 jelly roll pans or rimmed baking sheets with aluminum foil, spray each one with cooking spray then set aside.

2 Pour Bugles and nuts into a very large bowl and set aside. The bowl not only needs to be big enough to hold the ingredients, but should also have plenty of room to stir everything well without spilling it all over.

3 Add brown sugar, corn syrup, butter and ½ tsp salt to a medium-sized saucepan and place over medium heat. Stir the mixture constantly using a wooden spoon until it comes to a rolling boil. Remove the saucepan immediately from heat then pour the sugar mixture evenly over the Bugles and nuts. Stir with a wooden spoon until each piece is well coated in the mixture—you'll want to work fast because this stuff gets really sticky as it cools!

4 Divide the mixture in half and spread onto the 2 prepared baking sheets. Move both pans to the oven and bake for 15 minutes. Remove the mix from the oven and sprinkle with a little additional salt (if desired).

5 Allow the crunch to cool for a few minutes before breaking the clumps into pieces. Transfer this scrumptious mix to a large bowl and watch it disappear in a matter of moments!

prep time: 5 minutes

cook time: 5 minutes

bake time: 15 minutes

makes 15 cups sweet & salty crunch

what you'll need

12 cups Bugles corn snacks
   (2 - 14.5 oz bags)
3 cups assorted nuts (use whatever
   you like)
1 cup brown sugar, packed
1 cup light corn syrup
8 Tbsp (1 stick) unsalted butter
½ tsp salt
sprinkle of kosher or sea salt (optional)

helpful hints

Forget the candy thermometer for this recipe! If you prefer more "crunch" to your crunch, bake it a few minutes longer...but keep an eye on it!

Cooked sugar gets incredibly hot and can stick to your skin if spilled or splashed so be very careful when cooking!

ROSEMARY & HONEY FRUIT SALAD

Turn boring old fruit salad into a company-worthy dessert. I like to make my rosemary and honey fruit salad recipe then serve it in martini glasses—the presentation is stunning and it tastes great too!

let's do it

1 Pour the honey and water into a small saucepan then warm over medium heat. Meanwhile, gently bruise the rosemary leaves using a wooden spoon—make sure to bruise only the leaves and not the bitter-tasting stem.

2 Add rosemary to the saucepan, then bring the mixture to a boil. Reduce heat to medium-low then allow the ingredients to simmer for about 2 minutes until the liquid is reduced by half.

3 When the mixture has reduced, remove it from the heat and allow it to cool for 5 minutes—remove rosemary sprig and discard. Continue to cool syrup until it achieves room temperature.

4 Add fruit to a large glass bowl. Pour fresh lemon or lime juice over the fruit then drizzle with the syrup. Gently toss to combine. Cover the bowl and chill in the refrigerator until you're ready to serve.

 prep time: 10 minutes

 cook time: 10 minutes

 makes 9 cups

what you'll need

½ cup water

¼ cup light honey

3" sprig fresh rosemary

¼ cup fresh lemon or lime juice

3 kiwi, peeled and sliced

6 cups assorted berries, cut into bite-sized pieces

helpful hints

Bruising herbs helps to release their aromatic oils. To bruise herbs, place a bunch on a cutting board and gently rub them using a wooden spoon.

If you don't want to use honey, you can replace it with 1/3 cup of granulated sugar and decrease the water to 1/3 cup as well.

easy armadillo potatoes

homemade Italian soda

DIY Polaroid magnets

whoopie pie cake with marshmallow cream

INDEX

I would like to thank the CherylStyle and Najafi Companies staff for their participation in food testing and for their tremendous support in this effort; the Beisner, Mckibben, Sistrunk, Davis and Coffey clans for a lifetime of sharing recipes; and my awesome friends in Webb City, Missouri, for giving me that hard-working Midwest work ethic that helped to get this book to print.

And finally, this book would not be possible if my patient husband and children hadn't graciously eaten the same meals over and over again until I got these recipes just right. I love you!

CEO and publisher: Cheryl Najafi
Food Stylist: Bryan Haramoto
Recipe Inspiration: Debbie Evans
Production Director: Cari Oberfield
Editorial Support: Lenni Wilson and Erika Shafer
Copy Editor: Ashley Maynard
Proofreader: Ashley Maynard
Production Coordinator: Suzanne Bishop
Graphic Design: Audrey Pekala
Photo Retouching: Audrey Pekala
Digital Marketing Support: Annmarie Kennick
Kitchen Support: Kailey Fierro, Max Alvarez
Hairstylist: Mark Laposky
Make-up Artist: Zach Deboodt
Photography by Erika Shafer
Illustrations: Jon Arvizu, Trapdoor Studio
Cover Design: Audrey Pekala
Mechanical Support: Travis Craine

CherylStyle®
CherylStyle.com

This book was produced by:

CherylStyle
publishing

1562 First Ave. #205-3383
New York, NY 10028-4004
www.CherylStyle.com